MILE END'S STEAM FINALE

by Kenn Pearce

The '500' class had finished working the prestigious "Overland" expresses by the late 1950s, but on this 1949 day No.502 John Gunn *had brought in the "Overland" from Tailem Bend. Fuel and sand had been obtained and the fireman is about to replenish the 7000-gallon capacity tender with water from the adjacent column at Mile End.*
Photo: J.G. Southwell

MANY THANKS

Grateful thanks are extended to the following people who have assisted me in various ways in the compilation of this book: George Rogers, Frank Knowling, Jack Wright, Neil Head, Arthur Vivian, Rex Mathews, George Bishop, Bob Yates (who advised on glossary details), Des Atkins and Dave Parsons at Islington; John Southwell and Kim Bird (who helped on some details and tidied up my spelling!); Murray Billett, Ray Zeffert, John Wilson, Don Moyses, Bruce Bickmore, Owen Moyes and finally Steve McNicol.

Thanks must go to the staff at the State Library (always enormously helpful) and the librarian at the Railway's Institute. Also, to the State Transport Authority of South Australia.

© 1983 by the publisher: Railmac Publications,
   P.O. Box 290, Elizabeth, South Australia 5112.

Printed by Kitchener Press Pty. Ltd., 49 Wodonga St, Beverley, South Australia 5009

New Zealand distribution:
Brick Row Publishing Co. Ltd.
P.O. Box 190, Wellington N.Z.

U.K. distribution:
Becknell Books, P.O. Box 21, Kings Lynn,
Norfolk, England PE30 2QP

RMPN23

National Library of Australia card number and ISBN:
ISBN 0-949817-11-2

Front cover: 523 taking on fuel. Rear cover: 702 on pilot duty. Both photographs taken by George Bishop during 1963. Luckily 523 and 702 escaped the cutter's torch and are now preserved in the Mile End Railway Museum.

CONTENTS

Introduction 5
Mile End locomotive depots 6
Rail distances 7
Mile End locomotive depots c1930 (layout drawing) 8
Locomotives on the books 1957 9
    Locomotives condemned during 1957
Port Adelaide closure 10
Accident revue 13
Typical loadings 14
    Light engine running schedule, Defective stokers, Loadings around the Port
Typical workings 1958 16
Booking on and off 17
    Booking on, Booking off, Max. loads of coal on tenders, Coal gantries, Lighting up, Other
    Mile End staff, Turntable diameters and restrictions, The washer out, Cold wash, Hot wash
Locomotives on the books as at 1/1/60 25
Workshop visitors during 1960 26
    Explanation of services
Engine mileages 27
    Monthly mileages of engines allocated to Mile End 1960, Engines parked or stored 1960
    Mile End engine strength, Country depots, Cutting up
Incidents and Accidents 31

1961 32
    Annual mileages for 1961, Farewell for the '500' class
The last of the 'S' class 34
1962 34
    Annual mileages for 1962, Scrapping
1963 35
    Works visitors in 1963, Comings and goings, Cutting up, Annual mileages for 1963
1964 40
    Engine mileages for 1964, Tailem Bend, Scrapping, Steam retained turns
Testing of Boilers 43
Boiler Inspection Reports 46
1965 47
    Summary of S.A.R. broad gauge steam workings during 1965
1966 51
    Summary of mileages in 1966, Services and B.I.Ts, Engines condemned during 1966
1967 55
    Engine status, Condemned, Final monthly mileages of engines 1967, Islington works,
    Removal of locomotives from the roundhouse
The last of the big power 60
The Men of Mile End 62
Glossary of terms 65
Class histories 70
Class specifications 74
Bibliography 76

INTRODUCTION

Mile End roundhouse was already a 'graveyard' when I first ventured into its confines on a cloudy June afternoon in the late 1960s. Lines of condemned, rusting locomotives, crowded the outside area, while underneath its roof four of the remaining '520' class 4-8-4s and a few luckier Rx engines accumulated dust in the gloom. For most of the engines on shed it would be but a short wait before there was a final call to Islington workshops — not for a service or even a boiler inspection — but for cutting up. And even that final journey would not be made in dignity — in steam — but lifeless behind a diesel intruder that in most cases had replaced the condemned steam engine just a few years earlier.

Mile End's Steam Finale is not a day by day account of life at a large steam depot in South Australia, nor is it a year by year account over the final decade, though it is set out in a similar manner. Rather it is a review of some of the events that occurred in the period **1957-67**, and a review of some of the practices of operating steam engines, practices that now are little more than history.

Instead of restricting the text to Mile End alone I have also made mention of the country depots, which of course received allocations of Mile End locomotives. Although centres such as Tailem Bend and Terowie may nowadays have lesser significance, they witnessed the final regular operation of broad gauge steam in 1967 (Tailem Bend finally dispensing with its Rx shunters on December 1, 1967).

Mile End was not only Adelaide's, but also the state's major steam locomotive depot. When it closed on June 30, 1967, it not only signalled the imminent end of South Australian broad gauge steam, but also the end of an era. It was the end of an era in which South Australian Railways had modernised its system, so that by the end of the 1920s the state had some of the most modern locomotives of the time, serviced in modern depots and workshops. The revitalization of the railways allowed the state to proudly claim its locally built engines were the 'best in Australia'.

With the end of this era no more "Mountains" would take the turntable before heading off to Tailem Bend on a heavy freight, nor stately 'S' class would simmer in the afternoon sunshine waiting for a northbound roster to come their way. Those smoke-filled, but more leisurely, even nostalgic days are now, like the old roundhouse, gone forever.

Kenn Pearce
January 1982

Photo opposite: This impressive aerial shot gives a good indication of the roundhouse layout by 1965. Already sections of the 43 roads have been demolished, and rusting lines of condemned engines crowd the outside areas.
Photo: J. Wilson collection

MILE END LOCOMOTIVE DEPOTS

Islington was the main locomotive depot for the Adelaide district before the development of Mile End. Islington was opened in 1882 and operated until May 25, 1923, when it was closed. The Mile End goods yard development began in 1909, and by 1912 a seven-lane straight depot had been established near Railway Terrace, this opening on November 3 of that year. This depot was originally served by a 60 foot turntable until replaced with a 75 foot unit during the 1923-4 financial year, this being ten feet smaller than the unit eventually installed to service the roundhouse begun at this time.

Under the Webb modernisation plan for S.A.R. in the 1920s the reorganisation of motive power depots included the provision of roundhouses at Mile End and Tailem Bend, with a third roundhouse being planned, but never instigated, for Dry Creek yard. The departure from a 'straight-shed' philosophy was quite a radical move for the times, and on a few occasions, as teething problems occurred in all facets of the Webb programme, roundhouse opponents were able to mutter "We told you so."

Started in 1924 the Mile End round house was 'finished' by 1926, though it was recorded that the depot would be available for the stabling of engines from about July 1, 1925. In November 1924 £14,000 was reported having been spent on the depot, while the total cost was estimated to be in the order of £55,000 (estimate at November 20, 1924).

The coaling stage was finished by August 1925, though the turntable had yet to be completed (so any stabling of engines would not have been under cover of the 43 bays that made up the roundhouse). Double track ashpit, inspection pits, foreman's office and drop pits were still to be finished at this time, although mess rooms and sanitary accommodation had been completed.

Asphalt flooring had unwisely been used in the depot area at a cost of some £1,045, and soon proved to be inadequate for the heavy duty it received. This had to be taken up in part, and was replaced with concrete strip and glazed brick between the radial pits. The cost of these alterations — which raised a few eyebrows — totalled some £7,083. This was finished by August 1925.

Initial cost of the Webb rehabilitation scheme up to June 30, 1928 amounted to some £7,503,000, with additional loan works not strictly amounting to rehabilitation, a further £2,809,962. In the former figure was contained £379,000 for the provision of roundhouses, and this of course would include the Tailem Bend establishment.

Blow-down connections were completed at Mile End by September 1928, together with machines for the repair shop at the depot. By 1930 a water softening plant had been finished, together with the near completion of a new hot washout plant (the original washout plant being finished by August 1925) at a cost of £4,300.

During the Second World War the roundhouse was blacked-out for defence reasons, as were the engines that worked from there for a while.

Post-war, staffing was probably at its highest point, before the rot set in and staff started to be drawn away. By the mid-fifties about 430 men were estimated to be employed at the shed.

In 1957 there appear to have been efforts made to make the working environment a little more pleasant, no mean feat in a traditionally dirty, smoky surrounding, with the planting of a garden around the loco area beginning to take shape. At the same time the Roundhouse Social Club was providing social evenings for shed staff, their friends and families with films and talks of "instructional and educational" nature. On April 12, for example, about 320 people attended such a 'night out'.

By the early sixties employment at the depot had dropped to between 100 to 200 men, the biggest reduction starting with the transfer of many repair staff to Islington from the end of 1962, and the completion of facilities at Mile End diesel depot late in 1963.

With the gradual rundown of steam turns, and the influx of further diesels during 1964-7, the roundhouse was closed as of June 30, 1967 — the only staff then being a solitary caretaker. Control of the depot then fell under the foreman of Mile End diesel depot, about a quarter of a mile north of the roundhouse, and any steam rosters during the last months came from there.

The demolition of the giant coaling stage in the early 1970s caused some pausing for reflection by some of the shed staff who had coaled their charges beneath the concrete gantry, and was quite a talking point. The final demolition of the roundhouse took a little longer, and it wasn't until the mid-seventies that the final reminder of the age of steam had been removed.

A section of the Mile End roundhouse in the construction phase. The turntable, although delivered has yet to be installed.

RAIL DISTANCES

Throughout this book reference is made to various places on the South Australian Broad gauge system, some far more important in days gone by than today. As a quick guide, the below distances are given, all mileages are approximate, conversion to kilometres can be made by multiplying miles by 1.6.

Mile End to		Mile End to		Mile End to	
Victor Harbor	82¼ miles	Snowtown	89¾ miles	Gladstone	136¼ miles
Pooraka	8 miles	Redhill	106½ miles	Balaklava	66¾ miles
Terowie	139¾ miles	Angaston	51½ miles	Brinkworth	104¼ miles
Gawler	24¾ miles	Truro	58 miles	Tailem Bend	74¾ miles
Roseworthy	30½ miles	Morgan	104¾ miles	Murray Bridge	60 miles
Hamley Bridge	44½ miles	Robertstown	83 miles	Mt Barker Junction	31 miles
Riverton	63 miles	Eudunda	68¾ miles	Willunga	34¼ miles
Port Pirie Junction	134¼ miles	Spalding	115 miles	Moonta (via Hamley Bridge)	134½ miles
Long Plains	47 miles	Clare	90¾ miles	Belair	13½ miles
Bowmans	63 miles	Moonta	121¾ miles	Mt Lofty	19½ miles

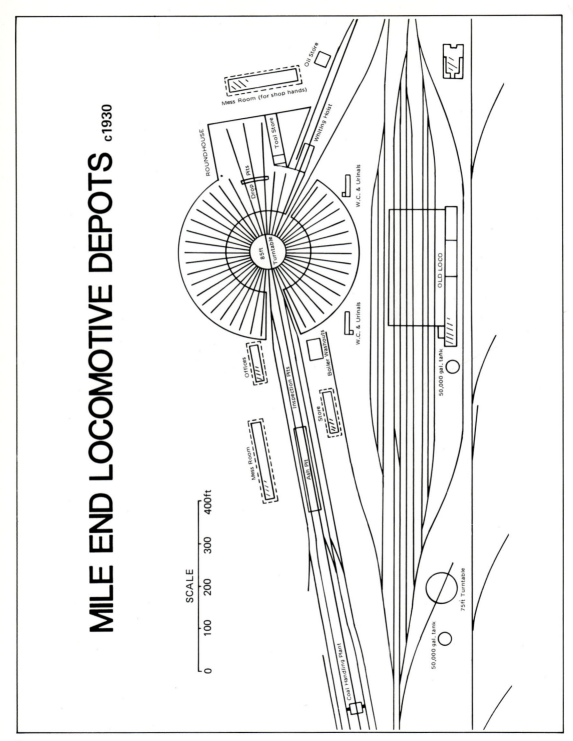

LOCOMOTIVES ON THE BOOKS 1957

The following engines were on South Australian Railways broad gauge register as of January 1, 1957. Not all engines would necessarily be trafficable.

2nd F class 4-6-2T

168	172	175	179	183	186	236	240	243	246	249	252
170	173	176	180	184	188	237	241	244	247	250	253
171	174	177	181	185	189	238	242	245	248	251	255

Total: 36

P class 2-4-0T

72 73 116 118 119 121 122 123 124

Total: 9

Rx class 4-6-0

5	48	140	190	195	201	208	213	218	224	230	235
9	55	146	191	197	202	209	214	219	225	231	
15	56	155	192	198	203	210	215	220	227	232	
20	93	158	193	199	206	211	216	221	228	233	
25	139	160	194	200	207	212	217	222	229	234	

Total: 56

S class 4-4-0

11 14 17 26 128 131 132 136

Total: 8

500 class 4-8-4

500 *James McGuire*
501 *Sir Henry Barwell*
502 *John Gunn*
503 *R.L. Butler*
504 *Tom Barr Smith*
505 *Sir Tom Bridges*
506 *Sir George Murray*
507 *Margaret Murray*
508 *Sir Lancelot Stirling*
509 *W.A. Webb*

Total: 10

520 class 4-8-4

520 *Sir Malcolm Barclay-Harvey*
521 *Thomas Playford*
522 *Malcolm McIntosh*
523 *Essington Lewis*
524 *Sir Mellis Napier*
525 *Sir Willoughby Norrie*
526 *Duchess of Gloucester*
527 *C.B. Anderson*
528
529
530
531

Total: 12

600 class 4-6-2

600 601 602 603 604 605 606 607 608
609 *Duke of Gloucester*

Total: 10

620 class 4-6-2

620 *Sir Winston Dugan*
621 622 623 624 625 626 627 628 629

Total: 10

700 and 710 class 2-8-2

700	703	706	709	712	714 *Rotarian*	717
701	704	707	710 *Sir Alexander Ruthven*			718
702	705	708	711	713	715 716	719

Total: 20

720 class 2-8-4

720	722	724	726	728	730	732	734	736
721	723	725	727	729	731	733	735	

Total: 17

740 class 2-8-2

740	741	742	743	744	745	746	747	748	749

Total: 10

750 class 2-8-2

750	751	752	753	754	755	756	757	758	759

Total: 10

Total locomotives: 208

Locomotives condemned during 1957
F247, F248, F252, P72, P73, P116, P118, P119, P121, P122, P123, P124, Rx220, Rx221, Rx234, S132.

PORT ADELAIDE CLOSURE

In July 1957 the metropolitan's other main steam depot, at Port Adelaide, was officially 'closed to steam'. This very old depot had become a part of the early Port Adelaide skyline and certainly was remembered by some railwaymen from the era when coppertops (highly polished) and shining brass were *demanded* by the authorities, and drivers would report to work in uniform of black shirts and white ties.

A traverser, located behind the freight office, permitted the release of locomotives after the arrival of the "Loopie" from Dry Creek. With the closure of the depot to steam the last 'P' class tank engines were also condemned, this class of engine had been retained there to the end for local shunting. Diesel locomotives were used from the depot, but also the shed provided a convenient storage area, before scrapping, of locomotives. For example, in 1959 two lines of condemned engines were adjacent to the coal gantry, comprising: F173, F175, F237, Rx206, F246, S11 (which had been yard shunter at Mile End during 1957), F183, F238, F242, S137, F243, S132, Rx203, S13 and S128.

By the late '60s Port Adelaide depot still retained a loco shed 'air', though by then it was being used as a private warehouse, windows having been boarded up and the pits filled. The depot still stands today.

P117 was the "Roundhouse Rat" at Tailem Bend in the mid-1950s. It was officially withdrawn on December 27, 1956. This engine is now preserved at Mile End Railway Museum.   Photo: J.G. Southwell

A feature of the Islington works annual picnic was the use of one or more steam hauled special trains. No.505 Sir Tom Bridges *urges a long rake of Centenary and end-loading cars upgrade on the main south line near Millswood in the mid-1950s.*
Photo: J.G. Southwell

Rx218 receives attention at Bridgewater in the 1950s. Note the small six-wheel tender often coupled to engines of this class to negotiate the smaller turntables. Locos would often be stabled at Bridgewater overnight, dropping their fire, and returning the following morning to Adelaide.
Photo: S.A. Archives

With the advent of the '520' class 4-8-4s the '600' class Pacifics tended to concentrate on the Murray Bridge Division working heavy passenger and freight trains to Serviceton, and later Mt Gambier. However, they sometimes made forays to Pt Pirie from where 608 has just arrived in 1956. This loco ran over a million miles during its lifetime.
Photo: J.G. Southwell

ACCIDENT REVUE

With such a large number of engines working from one engine-shed it was inevitable that there would be the occasional breakdown.

Despite constant checks and regularised servicing, engines would refuse to steam, run out of water, and in general prove a nuisance to public and crews alike.

Below are listed some typical engine ailments as recorded by one Mile End locomotive driver in the period 1954-1958, when diesel locomotives increasingly started to take over steam rosters.

March 8, 1954	Loco No.621 — steam pipe to whistle broke at Gawler en route to Gladstone. Replaced with engine No.627.
May 2, 1954	Rx48 — cowcatcher removed at Bowden, hit rail while shunting.
May 6, 1954	Loco No.736. Halved train between Callington and Waller en route to Tailem Bend. 435 tons.
October 2, 1955	Loco No.747 — lubricator pipe to left-hand cylinder broken, proceeded to Brinkworth, pipe welded.
October 16, 1955	Loco No.726. Left-hand trailing coupling rod broke, took rods off, replaced by engine No.716.
July 23, 1956	Loco No.732 collided with No.520 *Sir Malcolm Barclay-Harvey* at Snowtown, both damaged and derailed (fireman's error).
February 27, 1957	Loco No.621, fireman could not raise steam, 50 lb (per sq. in.) at time to leave. Left 83 minutes late with engine No.714.
May 17, 1957	Loco No.726 hot right-hand engine box smoking, replaced with No.625 at Gawler working home from Saddleworth.
September 9, 1957	Loco No.733 reach-rod uncoupled, worked engine to Bowmans from Kallora, took bolts from pressure gauge and coupled rod again, engine then went to Port Pirie.
April 1958	Rx218, both injectors failed, right-hand at North Adelaide, left-hand at Dry Creek. Knocked fire out, steamed back to Dry Creek, replaced with Rx190.
September 4, 1958	Loco No.508 *Sir Lancelot Stirling* air pipe in right-hand release cock broke working 621 down to Snowtown. Changed with No.504 *Tom Barr Smith* at Dry Creek. Loco No.504 *Tom Barr Smith* cap lost off reverse lever lubricating cap. Continued to Bowmans without cap.

Of the above incidents the collision between 732 and 520 at Snowtown in 1956 was caused by the fireman missing the 'stick' at red guarding 520 which was struck on the crossing. Both engines had some damage inflicted, though the culprit 732 came off worse, sustaining a few broken pipes, though nothing serious.

The incident was considered serious by rail authorities however, and for his pains the driver of the Berkshire was relegated to shunting duties for three months.

A driver was never penalised however for dropping his fire as occurred with Rx218 in April 1958 when both injectors failed. As one former Mile End driver explained, it was a serious matter to 'drop a plug', and it was dealt with by relegating a driver to fireman position for three months.

The main problem with defective injectors is that the engine will continue to blow-off, and a ¾-full glass can soon become half or even quarter full unless a decision is made quickly to remove the fire. A broken clack in *both* of Rx218's injectors was found to be her failing.

TYPICAL LOADINGS

Listed below are loads that were permitted to be hauled by engines working out of Mile End round-house. All weights are in tons; and are the maximum weight that could be hauled by a class member over ALL sections of a given route. (Engines could frequently haul much higher loads over limited sections of a given route.)

DOWN refers to trains working away from Mile End, while UP refers to trains working to Mile End. All tonnages are for engines hauling goods and livestock trains unless otherwise stated.

Route predom. gradient Class	Mile End-Gawler DOWN 1 in 160	UP 1 in 145	Gawler-Roseworthy DOWN 1 in 62	UP 1 in 92	Roseworthy-Terowie DOWN 1 in 90	UP 1 in 85	Mile End-Pt Pirie DOWN 1 in 100	UP 1 in 10
'F'	450	410	—	—	—	—	450[2]	410
'Rx'	550	550	340	510	495	460	550	550
'S'	320	370	260	370	320	320	340[3]	370
'P'	—	—	—	—	—	—	—	—
500	1800	2500	870	1260	1260	1100	—	—
500*	2000	2500	1040	1440	1450	1335	—	—
520	1160	1400	570	860	850	750	950	880
	450‡	450‡	450‡	450‡	450‡	450‡	500‡	500
600	1250	2500	620	930	890	860	1000	1000
	450‡	450‡	450‡	450‡	450‡	450‡	500‡	500
620	830	1000	410	615	610	540	680	685
700/710/740	1400	2500	710+	1000	935	870	1100	1100
720	1400	2500	710+	1025	950	885	1170	1170
720*	1610	2500	890+	1240	1150	1070	1400	1400
750	820	1200	510	760	620	610	820	825

Notes

* * Engines fitted with a booster
* ‡ Loadings for passenger trains
* \+ Loads of freight trains over the Gawler-Roseworthy section if a push engine (a banker) was attached at Gawler, this being an Rx loco. Weights then could be:
  720 class — 1050 tons
  720 class (booster) — 1230 tons
  700/710/740 class — 1050 tons.
  Push engines returning 'light' from Roseworthy were prohibited from exceeding 30 mph.
* † Tender-first working
* 1 Only Snowtown-Mile End section.
* 2 Only Mile End-Bowmans.
* 3 Only to Collinsfield (between Snowtown and Redhill)
* 4 Only Snowtown-Mile End.
* 5 Only Mile End-Glanville and Pt Adelaide-Glanville.
* 6 Only Mile End-Reynella.
* 7 Only Mile End-Mt Barker Junction section.
* 8 Mile End-Moonta via Hamley Bridge.

Mile End-Adelaide
Tonnages allowed between these two points, for short pickups or transfers was Rx class — 350 tons, F class — 330 tons.

Mile End-Terowie

Besides the normal Terowie freight services S.A.R. operated an express goods (train no.539) at 12.35pm every Monday, Wednesday and Friday which contained perishables for centres beyond Terowie (Broken Hill and even Quorn). This train commanded tighter schedules and reduced loadings for engines, and is given as an example of weight variations on rosters of a special nature. A favored roster for '520' class engines, others would be used from time to time.

Section	Class					TONS
	500	720	600	700	520	
Mile End to Riverton	800	600	600	500	480	TONS
Riverton to Terowie	700	550	550	450	480	

e End-Mt Lofty		Mt Lofty-Tailem Bend		Tailem Bend-Serviceton		Belair-Mile End		Mile End-Pt Ad.-Outer Hbr	
WN	UP	DOWN	UP	DOWN	UP	DOWN	UP	DOWN	UP
1 45	—	1 in 45	1 in 45	1 in 80	1 in 80	—	—	—	—
—	—	—	—	—	—	160	400	330	530
90	400	210	190	—	—	190	600	460	625
								390†	555†
20	120	120	120	—	—	—	—	295⁵	370⁵
—	—	—	—	—	—	—	—	225	375
00	1200	590	500	—	—	—	—	—	—
40	1200	700	540	—	—	—	—	—	—
70	805	270	270	900	940	—	—	—	—
70‡	270‡	270‡	270‡	500‡	500‡	—	—	—	—
50	805	400	350	950	1100	—	—	—	—
70‡	270‡	270‡	270‡	575‡	575‡	—	—	—	—
30	805	270	230	—	—	—	—	—	—
90	1200	450	390	950	1100	—	—	—	—
85	1200	450	385	950	1100	—	—	—	—
50	1200	570	450	1170	1120	—	—	—	—
85	1200	340	285	700	750	—	—	605	825
								512†	732†

Route	Mile End-Gladstone		Mile End-Willunga		Mile End-Victor Harbor		Mile End-Moonta (via Long Plains)	
predom. gradient	DOWN	UP	DOWN	UP	DOWN	UP	DOWN	UP
Class	1 in 90	1 in 90	1 in 52	1 in 62	1 in 62	1 in 58	1 in 97	1 in 98
'F'	—	—	190⁶	200⁶	—	—	—	—
'Rx'	340	360	220	220	190	190	325	380
'S'	235	235	120	150	120	120	210⁸	230⁸
'P'	—	—	—	—	—	—	—	—
500	—	—	—	—	500	500	—	—
500*	—	—	—	—	540	540	—	—
520	570	610	310	330	270	270	600	630
600	—	—	—	—	350	350	—	—
620	410	410	240	240	230	230	430	450
700/710/740	710	740	440	475	390	390	680	805
720	—	—	—	—	385	385	—	—
720*	—	—	—	—	450	450	—	—
750	510	550	300	300	285⁷	285⁷	480	560

Light engine running schedule:
Engines entering traffic were allowed three minutes between Mile End locoshed and Junction cabin, five minutes from Junction cabin and Adelaide station, and ten minutes from Mile End locoshed to the Goods Yard (via Keswick) which included advising the cabin of departure. Five minutes was allowed Junction cabin to the Goods Yard. Often engines would have to travel 'light' between Mile End and Dry Creek. 16 minutes was allowed for this short trip.

Engines entering the locoshed were allowed four minutes to travel from Adelaide station to Junction cabin (Mile End), four minutes for Junction cabin to Loco Pointsman's cabin, seven minutes from Goods Yard to locoshed, and six minutes from Goods Yard to beyond Junction cabin.

Defective stokers
Engines fitted with a mechanical stoker (coal only) in which the stoker was defective would be permitted to have train loads reduced to 75 per cent of non-booster loads for such schedules.

Coal-oil burning engines equipped with mechanical stokers would haul the full 100 per cent load irrespective of whether the stoker was operational or not.

Loadings around the Port
Loads for 'P' class shunting engines between Port Adelaide and Dock station and the wharves or marshalling yard.

Wharf or Station	Load
Berths Nos. 1, 2, 3, 4, 5 and 6	235 tons
Berths Nos. 8, 9, 10, 11 and 12	235 tons
Berths Nos. 13 and 14	235 tons
Berths Nos. 16 and 17	325 tons
Berths Nos. 18, 19 and 20 (south approach)	340 tons
Berth No. 20 (north approach)	340 tons
Between Gillman yard and Ocean Steamers' line	410 tons

TYPICAL WORKINGS 1958

During 1958 there still remained one or two turns that kept the Webb 'superpower' occupied, though their workings would be cut considerably the following year. As a guide to the type of rosters a Mile End driver would encounter during the last years of intensive steam working on the broad gauge, the below list is offered:

February 2, 1958	No.733 to Angaston	2317 hrs. on / 0830 hrs. off
February 3, 1958	returned	1645 hrs. on / 0045 hrs. off
February 4, 1958	No.F249 (suburban)	1458 hrs. on / 2052 hrs. off
February 5, 1958	No.733 to Snowtown	1630 hrs. on / 1230 hrs. off
February 6, 1958	No.733 (returns)	1400 hrs. on / 2330 hrs. off
February 12, 1958	No.743 to Melton	1908 hrs. on / 0358 hrs. off
February 13, 1958	No.743 (returns)	1430 hrs. on / 0140 hrs. off
April 14, 1958	No.733 to Riverton	1145 hrs. on / 1855 hrs. off

April 15, 1958	No. Rx25 returns from Riverton	1815 hrs. on
		0035 hrs. off
April 22, 1958	No.F255 (suburban)	0540 hrs. on
		1458 hrs. off
April 23, 1958	No.753 to Riverton	0615 hrs. on
		1455 hrs. off
April 24, 1958	No.722 returns from Riverton	0045 hrs. on
		0845 hrs. off
April 26, 1958	No.Rx211 (suburban)	0510 hrs. on
		1425 hrs. off

Of the above rosters, those of the '720' class are interesting because 1958 was to be almost the final full year in which the class was occasionally used. In fact looking at a former Mile End driver's roster sheet, only two workings involving a Berkshire were recorded for the latter part of 1958. No.735 was used to Dry Creek on June 9, and No.721 to Lyndoch on August 7.

The classes' imminent demise was confirmed as early as March 1958 when No.734 was condemned, followed by No.729 in August and No.725 in September. This engine became the first of its class to be cut up at Islington on October 30, 1958.

BOOKING ON AND BOOKING OFF

Starting work for an engineman, or finishing, required set procedures which even today are carried out. But in the days of steam it was not simply a case of starting up or turning off a diesel engine. In case booking on and booking off procedures in the days of steam might be forgotten, the following duties were set out for engine-crews working out of Mile End roundhouse. Minor variations occasionally occurred (such as taking coal on the way off shed) during the 1950s and 1960s.

Booking on

When a driver or fireman booked on he would look at the roster board to see what was his turn for the day, what engine was rostered, and in what lane to find it. The driver would go to the oil store and receive his allocation of cylinder and engine oil, a bucket, a broom, a slushy and signal lamp.

Over in the stall the driver would set to oiling the locomotive while the fireman checked the fire (already lit for him) and started to 'push it down'. After a brief examination over the pit the crew were given the turntable, and the loco would be turned in the direction needed to leave. The crew would then take water before leaving the yard to take up their freight or passenger consist. Crews could never be certain how long their 'turn' would last (particularly so in later years when various standards of coal made fire-cleaning a regular task) though pilot duty was usually a straight eight hour shift. Nevertheless, as pilot the crew had to be prepared to 'go away' should the need arise.

Booking off

This was the best part of the engineman's shift, particularly if he was returning to Mile End. But it would be wrong to assume the crew simply uncoupled from their train, ran to shed and signed off. Up to an hour later the crew might be 'putting their charge to bed'.

With a '720' class engine, for example, 55 minutes was allowed for the driver to stable his engine after coming off a train, the fireman being allowed 45 minutes. Different engine classes were allowed different times (commensurate with size) and similarly a '520' class loco would be permitted 60 minutes to be stabled.

After being uncoupled from their train the crew would take their engine past the points, where the pointsman would sign the engine in. Usually a little bit of friendly haggling would go on here, as the driver might attempt to get an extra minute out of the precise timekeeping pointsman. The crew were then allowed eight minutes to go across Mile End yard to the engine-shed, where the first task would be to fill the engine's sandboxes. Coal would usually be taken then (at least during the 1950s) and some engines would have to be moved two or three times in order to distribute the coal evenly in the tender. The size of bunkers on some engines (including the 2nd Fs) often meant more coal would appear to be on the ground than in the engine, and on more than one occasion the coal chute failed to shut off, partially burying an engine below!

Water would then be taken, and the fire would be cleaned over the drop pit (judicious use of a hose on the ashpan would enable a driver to clean both sides from the one spot).

An oil burner would take oil first, and then if needed, coal from the gantry.

Then the driver would examine his engine over the examination pit. The things he would be looking for would include broken springs, shock absorbers, leaking water pipes or steam coming out from underneath boiler clothing (indicating possibly a broken stay). He would also check the ashpan area; checking the slides to ensure they were clear, and he would ask the fireman to close them once he had made an inspection. The driver would also look for loose bolts. Faults were recorded on a repair sheet approximately 10" x 8" in size. The foreman fitter could then hand this on to repair staff to attend to. About 20 to 25 fitters, together with their mates, were employed at the roundhouse in the period being covered.

Brakes were always adjusted on return to Mile End, irrespective of whether they needed attention or not. Used blocks were saved on a pile, and eventually sent to Islington for melting down and recasting.

The loco marshaller would take over custody of an incoming engine, once the driver had made his inspection. The engine would then be put in a predetermined stall.

Engine crews would work a 'link', comprised of a 50-week roster. By this method a driver could determine what turn he was likely to be given in the coming weeks, simply by looking at corresponding periods last year.

F180 below the Mile End coal gantry in the mid-1950s.   Photo: S.A. Archives

Maximum loads of coal on tenders					
Type	80lb rail	60lb rail	Type	80lb rail	60lb rail
500 class	11ton (275 baskets)	—	Ordinary bogie	7.825ton (195 bkts.)	7.825ton (195 bkts.)
520 class	7ton (175 bkts.)	5ton (125 bkts.)	6-wheel self-trim	6.825ton (170 bkts.)	6.825ton (170 bkts.)
600 class	12ton (300 bkts.)	—	Small 6-wheel	5.625ton (140 bkts.)	5.625ton (140 bkts.)
620 class	9ton (225 bkts.)	9ton (225 bkts.)	F class	2.25 ton (56 bkts.)	2.25 ton (56 bkts.)
700/710 class	17ton (425 bkts.)	14½ton (362 bkts.)	P class	1.5 ton (38 bkts.)	1.5 ton (38 bkts.)
720 class	17ton (425 bkts.)	—			

The above tonnages represent the maximum permitted loads in the corresponding tenders. In addition, engines when stabled at Mile End needed extra coal added to the tender for lighting up purposes:

    Large power (excluding 620 class)   — extra 31 baskets.
    620 class   — extra 20 baskets.
    Rx and S class   — an additional 5 baskets.

Engines of 700/710 class rostered for pilot on the Willunga line only coaled to 14.5 tons plus 31 baskets for light up. 720 class working wayside freights, Mile End to Terowie, were coaled to 20 tons (500 baskets) immediately before leaving Mile End roundhouse.

700/710 class working wayside freights, Mile End to Morgan, were coaled to 19 tons (475 baskets) immediately before leaving Mile End. The engines were required to fill their tenders at Gawler, but were forbidden to take water at Roseworthy.

Engines were not to be coaled when stabled at Wallaroo, and were required to take only sufficient coal when leaving loco in order to perform their roster.

All loads were subject to modification following conversion to coal/oil burning.

Coal gantries

Nine coal-handling plants were ordered from the U.S.A. firm of Roberts & Schaefer in Chicago as part of the Webb modernisation programme in the early 1920s. Mile End coal gantry was recorded as completed in the Commissioner's report for 1924-5, while the status of other gantries was recorded as:

Port Adelaide	(150 tons capacity) nearly completed, machinery not yet installed.
Tailem Bend	(300 tons cap.) concrete structure completed but machinery not yet installed.
Peterborough	(300 tons cap.) structure in progress.
Gladstone	Excavations in progress, no concrete work undertaken.
Port Pirie	(500 tons cap.) This plant was of a different type, the tower being separate from the main structure. Excavation for the main pit has been completed and partly concreted superstructure not yet begun.
Wallaroo	(150 tons cap.) site not finalised.
Karoonda	(150 tons cap.) site not finalised.

Besides the above, an Adelaide gantry was envisaged of 150 tons capacity. Because of the remodelling then in progress in Adelaide yard, the gantry's construction was held in abeyance.

The Wallaroo coal stage had been completed by September 1927, and was quite a landmark in the area until demolished in the mid 1970s despite protestations that it should be kept as a historical piece. Terowie did not receive its smaller coal stage until the Second World War period, and only after complaints by crews of hand coaling. Acquisition of the necessary machined parts for the stage further delayed its early commission. Small wooden coal stages also existed at other important lineside locations, including Riverton.

Lighting-up

One of the less glamorous tasks at any locomotive depot in the days of steam was that of lighter-up. These were people assigned to raising steam from the cold, or sometimes warm, engines to be used for the day. At Mile End, when steam was still being used frequently, a fire would never be dropped when an engine had no mechanical defects to be attended to. This saved both fuel and time in the case of emergency rostering of a stabled engine.

Two men were assigned to lighting-up duties on each shift, while another would have the job of loading up cab floors with wood to get the fires going. Lighters-up (who had to have a boiler attendant's certificate) would first check that there was enough water in the boiler, at least 1-1½" in the gauge glass. If there wasn't enough, the washer-out would be called in to stick a hose up the blow-off pipe, the blow-off cock would be opened and the boiler was then replenished.

A stick wrapped in a kerosene rag was lit and dropped in the firebox, and the kindling wood would then be loaded onto the small fire. Once a reasonable fire was going, small sized coal pieces could be introduced. Thus the lighter-up went from engine to engine, a tedious task climbing up and down cab steps of 20 or 30 locos at the eerie hour of perhaps 1 am or 2 am.

When an engine started to make enough steam the lighter-up could use the engine's blower, which enabled a vacuum to be created, and the thick smoke from the fire was then directed out through the chimney rather than the firebox door. Once a good head of steam had been raised, a good portion of coal would be left just inside, and underneath, the firebox door. Towards the end of steam the lighters-up started to use an oil-blower which greatly speeded up their task. This was really similar to a flame-thrower; fires were usually saved unless an engine specifically had to be cooled.

Although crews would have their engine already prepared for them S.A.R. did stipulate time allowances for lighting-up, when away from home depot. Times allowed are on the below chart.

Class	Time allowed	
a. Cold Rx, S.F.	3 hours	In all cases these allowances include time allowed for preparation of the engine. Engines were regarded as "warm" up to 16 hours after fire had been drawn in the case of small engines *vide a* and *b* in the above table, and 24 hours in the case of others. The period in all cases being calculated from 15 minutes after the engines concerned arrive on the pit for the purpose of stabling.
b. Warm Rx, S.F.	2½ hours	
c. Cold 620 class	5 hours	
d. Warm 620 class	3¾ hours	
e. Cold 500, 520, 600, 700, 710, 720, 740, 750 classes	6 hours	
f. Warm 500, 520, 600, 700, 710, 720, 740, 750 classes	3 hours	

Other Mile End staff
An important employee at any roundhouse is the turntable operator. At the Mile End roundhouse the turntable assistant worked an eight hour shift. In quiet periods he would employ himself greasing the undergear of the table, and fill sandboxes on the table to prevent it slipping in wet conditions. Sometimes the person allotted to this duty had a partial disability that prevented him from carrying out other depot tasks. Shifts were usually 7 am-3 pm, 3 pm-11 pm and 11 pm-7am.

> Two stop boards, each inscribed 'Stop' and provided with a red light for night indication, are installed on the turntable at the opposite end to the control cabin. The boards are located on each side of the turntable track, and the boards are visible only on the approach to the turntable this end.
>
> The turntable locking device must be in a locked position, i.e. plunged at the end of the turntable to be traversed by an engine moving to or from the turntable.
>
> Engine movements onto the turntable, except as described in the next paragraph, must be made from the control cabin end under the hand-signal green flag by day, green light by night — displayed by the turntable attendant after he has set and plunged the turntable.
>
> When it is necessary to move a dead engine from the bay of the Round-house, the dead engine and the engine under steam must be piloted onto the turntable from the end opposite to the control cabin. The movement must be made past the stop boards under the direction of the Shed Marshaller, who must first receive the 'all clear' signal from the turntable attendant.

Engine movements off the turntable must not be made until a hand-signal is received from the Turntable Attendant, who, after having set and plunged the turntable, must exhibit a green flag by day and a green light by night.

These somewhat thorough instructions were necessary to avoid a nightmare situation in railway operation, where a loco could become derailed on the turntable, or worse still even end up in the table pit, thereby rendering engines within the roundhouse isolated from their rostered duties. Such 'horror' derailments were rare if not totally unknown, but still provided 'straight-shed' adherents with their strongest criticism of roundhouse design.

The fitter's greaser would service the grease pads underneath the locos, which were removable and could be replaced. Grease nipples would also be attended to. These were sited on the big-ends and coupling rods. Three or four men were employed simply on greasing duty in each shift.

The marshaller took control of locos when crews brought in their engines before booking off (see page 17) and it was his job to put the engine on the table and allot the loco to its prescribed stall. At weekends, however, engines sometimes had to be stabled over near the drop pits, and sometimes two rows between the roundhouse and the straight shed were also fitted with stabled engines.

The men assigned to the coaling stage had a grimy, and in winter an often wet job, and unlike other shed staff were members of the Australian Railways Union. The mechanised function of the coal stage removed most of the manual work, but the use of stokers on some 'big power' necessitated some timely hammer blows to some of the larger lumps of coal that failed to drop through the coal screens.

Mile End also boasted its own 'chemist' in the form of a water analyst. He used to take water samples from locos to a shed near the oil store, to check for hardness or solids in the water. Records would be made against each engine, and doping of engine with anti-hardener was the solution. The material used, "a black substance, horrible stuff — it smelt awful too," was an improvement on what engine crews used in earlier times. Then they had simply added olive oil to water by way of the water gauge glasses!

Next to the water analyst's hut was the tool store, where shovels, tongs and other implements for re-arranging the fire could be obtained.

Mikado No.718 takes the turntable at Mile End on June 12, 1965.   Photo: J. Wilson

Turntable diameters and restrictions					
Location	Diameter/operation	Classes permitted	Location	Diameter/operation	Classes permitted
Aldgate	53' (manual)	All small power	Port Pirie Junc.	85' (power)	All classes
Angaston	60' (manual)	All small power	Strathalbyn	53' (manual)	All small power
Balaklava	85' (power)	All classes	Tanunda	53' (manual)	All small power
Belair	50' (manual)	Rx and S with 6-wheel tender only, F and P	Terowie	60' (manual)	All small power
			Victor Harbor	85' (power)	All classes
			Wallaroo	85' (power)	All classes
Bridgewater	85' (power)	All classes	**Murray Bridge division:**		
Brinkworth	85' (power)	All classes			
Burra	60' (manual)	All small power	Barmera	53' (manual)	All small power
Clare	53' (manual)	All small power	Mantung	50' (manual)	Rx and S with 6-wheel tender only, F and P
Eudunda	60' (manual)	All small power			
Gladstone	85' (power)	All classes			
Hamley Bridge	53' (manual)	All small power	Murray Bridge	53' (manual)	All small power
Islington	53' (manual)	All small power	Renmark	75' (manual)	All small power, 620 and 700 classes
Kapunda	60' (manual)	All small power			
Marino	60' (manual)	All small power	Tailem Bend	85' (power)	All classes
Milang	60' (manual)	All small power	Waikerie	53' (manual)	All small power
Mile End	85' (power)	All classes	Wolseley	75' (manual)	All small power, 620, 700 and 710 classes
Moonta	85' (power)	All classes			
Morgan	60' (manual)	All small power			
Port Adelaide	50' (manual)	Rx and S with 6-wheel tender only, F and P			

Note: Small power in this chart refers to F, P, Rx and S classes.

Office of the Loco. Foreman
Mile End 14-5-57   WHS/FR

SHED FOREMAN (ACTG.) MR. A.R. VIVIAN
SUB. FOREMAN J. DIXON, H. SELLARS, E. WEBSTER, A. PLATTEN, T. HEAD, E. FISK, K. BRAKENRIDGE.
RUNNING SHIFT FOREMEN   R.P. SURMAN, E.G. OVERALL, HARLEY E.C.G. SCOBLE, W. ALLEN.
PILOT CREWS.

PLEASE NOTE THAT WHEN THE FIRE OF THE PILOT ENGINE, USING COAL AND OIL FUEL, NEEDS REPLENISHING, COAL IS TO BE USED AS THERE IS A DANGER OF THE TUBES BEING FOULED IF THE OIL IS USED WHEN AN ENGINE IS STANDING.

(Signed) W.H. SHARD
ACTG. LOCO. FOREMAN.

Pilot staff at the depot were rostered for the occasional breakdowns that occurred from time to time, and usually were at the amenities room until summoned by the Running Shed Foreman on the loudspeaker. So many men were rostered for the north pilot, and usually an equal mount for the south, and the suburban. They would be sometimes called to take out the steam breakdown crane when a derailment occurred. One of the superintendents, and a man on the crane, beside the boiler attendant on the steam crane would go out. The latter would be raising steam (which took about an hour) as the pilot crew marshalled the breakdown consist. 700, 500, Rx and F or even 750 class locos would be used as pilots, though in later years 520 class engines found some of their last rosters on such mundane duty.

The Washer-Out
This person was responsible for ensuring engines received a regular boiler wash out at predetermined mileages. Engines out of service could also require a wash out at different intervals to prevent the build up of sludge and scale. The washer out had to have his competence assessed by the Locomotive Foreman, whose ultimate responsibility was the maintenance of the locomotive fleet.

Once a boiler was emptied for any reason a "boiler empty" sign would be attached to the engine, and was only removed by the washer out or lighter up, once he had checked it had been filled.

Hot water was used to wash out engines that were still 'warm', that is were still warm to the touch, while cold water was used to wash out engines that had cooled sufficiently, to avoid boiler damage.

Cold wash

Washout plugs would be removed, water would be played on all accessible inside areas (firebox crown sheet from front to back) working the mud and scale from the crown sheet towards the side and back water spaces, preventing it from being left on rear ends of flues and tubes.

The crown sheet and rear end of flues and tubes could be cleaned by means of plug holes in the back plate. The side spaces down to foundation ring would be washed, then the barrel. Soft metal rods and scrapers were used if stubborn scale or sludge had to be dislodged. After washing all water spaces would be examined with the aid of a light, and the boiler had to be passed as clean by the supervising boilermaker before plugs could be replaced. Once replaced, the boiler was immediately refilled, and if the engine was needed urgently it could be filled with hot water to speed up its return to traffic.

Hot wash

Engines could not have more than 90 lbs of pressure, with at least half a glass of water when handed over on the ashpit. The injectors were to be kept on until they ceased to operate, the boiler, on the by then stabled engine, should have at least a full glass of water and the pressure should be about 40 lbs per sq inch, the ideal conditions being as much water and as little steam as possible.

Steam would be blown down until no pressure remained in the boiler, blowing down to be not less than two hours. Once all steam pressure had gone, and temperature didn't exceed 120°F, it could be washed hot. After washing out was completed, the boiler examined and passed clean by the supervisor, it would immediately be refilled with hot water at 180°F from the roundhouse filling line.

Minimum time allowed for raising steam after a wash out was put at one hour, if it had been washed hot, and three hours if washed cold. Too fast raising of steam in a locomotive boiler could create stresses on the boiler resulting ultimately in damage.

Mile End loco depot had already begun to show signs of neglect due to the effects of dieselisation late in 1958. Racy-looking light Pacific No.625 was one bright spot though as her fireman filled the tender before working the afternoon passenger service to Tailem Bend.
Photo: J.G. Southwell

In the mid-fifties the '710' class were no strangers to working Tailem Bend rosters. Here No.716 passes Blackwood with such a train in 1956.
Photo: J.G. Southwell

LOCOMOTIVES ON THE BOOKS AS AT 1/1/60

The below list is of engines on the broad gauge steam register at the start of 1960. Not all of these locomotives were actually in use, and in fact a number would have seen little, if any, service. Locomotives of the Rx, 2nd F, 520, 700/710 and the 740 classes were types that were particularly useful at this period.

Rx class, 4-6-0

5	48	140	190	195	201	210	216	224	230
9	55	146	191	197	202	211	217	225	231
15	56	155	192	198	207	212	218	227	232
20	93	158	193	199	208	214	219	228	233
25	139	160	194	200	209	215	222	229	235

Total: 50

2nd F class, 4-6-2T

168	172	176	180	184	189	240	245	250	255
170	173	177	181	185	236	241	246	251	
171	174	179	183	188	237	244	249	253	

Total: 28

S class, 4-4-0

17   26   136

Total: 3

500 class, 4-8-4

500 *James McGuire*
502 *John Gunn*
503 *R.L. Butler*
504 *Tom Barr Smith*
505 *Sir Tom Bridges*
506 *Sir George Murray*
508 *Sir Lancelot Stirling*
509 *W.A. Webb*

Total: 8

520 class, 4-8-4

520 *Sir Malcolm Barclay-Harvey*
521 *Thomas Playford*
522 *Malcolm McIntosh*
523 *Essington Lewis*
524 *Sir Mellis Napier*
525 *Sir Willoughby Norrie*
526 *Duchess of Gloucester*
527 *C.B. Anderson*
528
529
530
531

Total: 12

600 class, 4-6-2

603   606   608

Total: 3

620 class, 4-6-2

| 620 *Sir Winston Dugan* | 624 | 626 | 628 |
| 621 | 622 | 623 | 625 | 627 | 629 |

Total: 10

700 and 710 class, 2-8-2

700	704	708	711	713	715	716	717
701	705	709	712	714 *Rotarian*		718
702	706	710 *Sir Alexander Ruthven*			719

Total: 18

720 class, 2-8-4

721   722   724   726   735   736

Total: 6

740 class, 2-8-4

740   741   742   743   744   745   746   747   748   749

Total: 10

750 class, 2-8-2
750 751 752 753 754 755 756 757 758 759

Total: 10

Total steam locomotives: 158

WORKSHOP VISITORS DURING 1960

January
Rx232 ('C service,) 700 (out of use), 520 (stored in erecting shop), F168 (frac cyl.)

February
524 ('C' service), Rx192 ('D' service), Rx229 ('D' service), 701 ('D' service)

March
... still there: 524, Rx229, 701, Rx158 ('C' service)

April
... still there: Rx158, Rx198, Rx48 ('D' service), F172 ('D' service), Rx193 ('D' service)

May
... still there: F172, Rx193, Rx198, Rx191 ('D' service), 521 ('D' service)

June
Rx212 ('D' service), 744 ('D' service), 522 F168 ('D' service),

July
... still there: F168, F185 ('D' service), Rx231 ('D' service), 522 ('D' service), 743 ('D' service)

August
... still there: F185, Rx231, Rx5 ('D' service), Rx160 ('D' service), F181 ('D' service), Rx230 ('D' service), 747 ('D' service)

September
... still there: F181, Rx230, F171, 714 ('D' service), Rx228 ('C' service), 523 ('D' service)

October
... still there: F171, 714, Rx228

November
Rx200 ('D' service)

December
... still there Rx200, F179 ('D' service), 500 ('D' service), Rx202 ('D' service), Rx207 (general overhaul), Rx218 ('D' service), F244 ('C' service)

Explanation of services

'A' service	5,000 miles (small power)	6,000 miles (large power)*
'B' service	10,000 miles (small power)	12,000 miles (large power)
'C' service	20,000 miles (small power)	24,000 miles (large power)
'D' service	40,000 miles (small power)	48,000 miles (large power)

An 'A' service would entail fairly minor details such as air filter, Pyle lighting, with axlebox wedges and valves and pistons being checked twice in this cycle. A 'D' service would be generally more thorough and would include check and repair parts such as rods, wheels, axles and boxes, safety valves, booster and stoker (where fitted). Boiler inspection tests were usually carried out at the 'D' stage. General overhauls were less frequent occurences, and generally came round about every six years. Sequence of servicing: A,B,A,C,A,B,A,D.

In this survey period 'small power' (in relation to service schedules) includes F, P, Rx, S, 500 and 720 class locos. Large power encompassed 600, 620 and the Mikado types. *The 520 class, as a result of their modern design features, were allowed intervals of 7000, 14000, 28000 and 56000 miles between A to D services.

Tailem Bend carried out 'A' to 'C' services on its allocated engines, and B.I.T.'s until 1963, when engines went to Islington for all but 'A' services. Because 'D' services were only carried out at the works, the appearance of Pacifics 600, 604, 607 and 608 'in town' from the Bend was indeed a rare sight.

Mile End roundhouse carried out 'A' and 'B' services and B.I.T.'s until the start of 1963 when it only carried out the light 'A' service.

ENGINE MILEAGES

The Mechanical Branch of South Australian Railways kept daily mileage records of all steam engines in service and had them recorded on sheets approximately 43cm x 30cm in size, that would cover a year's service. Record would also be made of services carried out during the year together with previous years' services; the forthcoming boiler inspection date would also be recorded here. Engines allocated to broad gauge country depots would also have their records maintained from Mile End depot, the only exception appearing to be Tailem Bend, which kept its own sheets.

Monthly mileages of engines allocated to Mile End, 1960:

Engine No.	Jan	Feb	March	April	May	June	July	August	Sept	Oct	Nov	Dec	TOTAL
Rx5	760	950	1195	890	1015	725	470	*	385	695	195	Sn	7280
Rx9	at Tailem Bend until July						175	1075	775	935	820	425	4205
Rx15	460	*	*	520	955	1020	1270	1100	1100	1400	1120	1165	10110
Rx93	390	1220	260	450	975	720	1430	985	1215	595	950	775	9965
Rx146	935	885	1390	1155	400	655	1345	705	165	885	1110	455	10085
Rx158	955	1110	*	530	910	1240	1115	175	180	190	850	270	7525
Rx160	3280	3525	2685	3290	2400	1260	185	*	1005	1135	355	205	19325
F168	285	45	1225	880	835	*	120	1110	535	575	365	785	6760
F170	845	1030	1345	810	940	965	165	90	515	540	695	1315	9255
F171	380	865	1045	785	1940	960	820	195	*	470	600	465	8525
F172	850	1320	435	*	805	1020	905	725	460	460	635	720	8335
F174	965	610	1195	770	975	1035	950	525	120	755	490	750	9140
F179	755	995	1070	835	785	1055	775	765	670	—	—	*	7705
F180	790	1255	*	40	1095	990	835	290	560	765	120	420	7160
F181	805	940	1230	950	750	840	805	*	180	1095	605	1115	9315
F185	1105	685	1090	840	880	455	*	90	810	540	920	—	7415
Rx190	1250	1370	1420	1095	1160	1335	420	985	1130	290	565	1075	12095
Rx191	175	160	1450	1065	140	1165	1380	1100	1050	1405	1120	560	10770
Rx192	1150	*	1120	1070	855	950	1055	1370	1350	1090	1335	330	11675
Rx193	1665	730	590	*	435	570	375	385	390	525	625	870	7160
Rx194	2420	2000	1960	2650	1860	1090	875	690	715	540	540	—	15340
Rx195	1265	770	1210	1110	705	840	945	1000	1300	820	1225	900	12090
Rx197	1130	1030	1135	250	875	1120	965	985	1305	1030	880	885	11590
Rx198	1095	—	*	*	350	840	1035	760	710	765	1035	485	7075
Rx199	60	765	1245	1040	825	1145	1240	890	1540	1080	905	635	11370
Rx200	1430	980	1205	1260	940	650	945	890	580	—	*	566	9446
Rx207	at Tailem Bend until 26/7/60						80	1000	925	955	590	*	3550
Rx209	at Tailem Bend until 14/7/60						440	385	630	475	1180	—	3110
Rx210	at Tailem Bend until 14/7/60						280	560	790	820	940	455	3845
Rx211	940	1485	645	400	1485	970	1030	1095	680	410	1235	925	11300
Rx212	715	1565	1640	800	665	*	545	710	860	760	90	50	8400
Rx215	1550	1250	1585	830	965	650	925	1150	710	1540	1385	975	13515
Rx218	1245	180	1640	970	830	1320	1600	1435	1325	1490	—	*	12035
Rx222	1175	1260	1530	635	555	830	1440	615	1000	1125	285	1230	11680
Rx224	—	—	—	—	*	—	75	525	660	565	1175	685	3685
Rx225	2130	1980	2090	2580	1120	785	805	290	380	825	1220	590	14795
Rx228	735	890	1300	1045	1665	865	1295	650	*	*	1795	1110	11350
Rx229	575	*	360	1155	695	875	730	395	550	445	560	765	7105
Rx230	595	985	1260	1175	585	565	465	*	*	480	805	495	7410
Rx231	750	515	950	530	610	210	*	355	540	700	450	735	6345
Rx232	—	870	1020	885	660	620	740	150	685	800	590	280	7300
Rx233	2500	2010	2070	2580	790	—	730	665	1335	1215	1155	645	15695
F236	1010	660	1195	455	—	—	—	555	70	—	490	1065	5500
F240	765	660	990	1035	830	1055	1040	1180	865	645	790	230	10085
F244	1060	980	860	1135	1005	950	720	730	530	75	—	*	8045

Engine No.	Jan	Feb	March	April	May	June	July	August	Sept	Oct	Nov	Dec	TOTAL
F249	785	445	—	920	980	755	570	810	850	475	760	400	7750
F250	735	535	1130	1135	1035	860	870	890	565	440	580	260	9035
F251	800	740	1145	995	970	990	580	465	305	390	725	160	8265
F253	825	690	1115	880	1055	975	765	1100	660	275	560	140	9040
F255	750	815	1110	805	325	—	—	290	620	615	760	680	6770
500	1090	1060	1930	1735	1700	1260	410	1400	1570	900	—	*	13055
504	—	—	—	—	—	—	—	—	—	—	1110	1110	2220
505	Locomotive to be stored when next due for general overhaul						930	1550	410	1505	1480	1130	7005
508	620	1005	310		1185	1180	765	1100	1135	780	1710	1320	11110
509	775	365	1225	1390	465	855	155	—	—	stored from 27/9/60			5230
521	570	895	560		155	1430	1275	2160	2055	1455	1675	1915	14145
522	280	—	—	—	—	*	385	1810	1250	1550	1950	2145	9370
523	1135	440	1400	2270	915	1910	600	*	915	1120	1910	1610	14225
524	—	*	1845	1690	2250	1495	980	855	1925	1995	1765	1770	16570
526	—	—	—	—	905	445	*	1770	1665	950	3280	1350	10365
529	400	...engine then stopped due to crown stay attention needed											400
530	...engine at Mt Gambier...						510	745	1945	1330	475	—	5005
531	695	—	1885	1170	1975	1335	1720	80	—	—	—	—	8860
621	—	—	155	1015	1375	505	580	—	1710	—	1030	—	6370
623	—	—	160	170	1160	—	—	...transferred to Tailem Bend					1490
624	—	—	—	—	—	—	—	—	—	—	590	160	750
625	—	—	—	—	—	—	—	—	—	—	505	340	845
627	—	—	875	—	530	290	220	175	—	—	—	—	2090
700	*	*	*	*	*	*	*	*	*	*	375	220	595
701	230	*	—	—	—	—	—	—	—	—	395	695	1320
706	—	355	545	795	1375	155	545	240	225	295	1695	650	6875
708	605	965	1185	1035	695	870	120	—	150	200	465	570	6860
740	1015	1150	—	—	—	140	1120	1140	1310	795	1230	—	7900
741	1230	1305	1540	675	1395	1590	2130	2210	1575	1650	735	—	16035
742	1560	100	2000	1770	780	1850	2440	1510	1950	1235	1380	1140	17715
743	1995	2240	1745	1745	710	—	100	1100	1760	1350	1490	1410	15645
744	730	2095	2500	1850	—	*	1390	1440	2070	935	815	1390	15215
745	1615	450	1200	1435	1595	1240	1180	1170	1410	—	—	—	11295
746	575	—	100	1630	1790	1350	1700	1660	1545	1000	2180	50	13580
747	505	1055	2005	1535	1570	—	*	570	1020	850	1350	785	11245
748	—	1265	1195	1200	1805	1190	1545	1610	1450	925	1555	1520	15260
749	1400	1620	1435	1290	1275	1655	1255	2140	790	1480	1815	1890	18045
752	970	2230	1990	1090	445	560	965	1565	1455	990	540	865	13665
756	—	—	—	410	...stored from 22/4/60								410
757	...at Tailem Bend					75	...stored from 27/6/60						75
759	2090	1150	1240	1030	1125	925	270	—	—	—	150	290	8270

Abbreviation: * *indicates engine was in the workshops.   Sn: at Snowtown*

Notes on the above mileages

Unfortunately some records of Rx and 710 class engines were unavailable for the year 1960. 2nd F tank F 177 (not included in the previous list) was shunter at Islington workshops until December 1960, when it was condemned. Engines: Rx208, Rx216, Rx217, 622, 626 and 755 were all allocated to Tailem Bend depot throughout the year and had their records kept there. The mileage for No.752 in August was notable in that the engine worked 27 out of 31 days of the month. No mileage was recorded for Rx202 until it was sent to Terowie on 30/12/60.

Engines 'parked' or stored during 1960

Decisions were made to 'park' or store the following engines during 1960, most would never steam again, being effectively surplus to requirements and a source of spare parts for the operating members in their class.

January   : 503 (having worked only 155 miles the previous year)

	520 (stored in the erecting shop at Islington works)	May	: 528 stored May 1960 622 parked 18/5/60
	525 also at Islington	June	: 626 parked 27/6/60
	629 last worked 29/9/59		757 parked 27/6/60
	750 stored 4/1/60	August	: 531 stored 10/8/60
February	: 529 stored after return from Mt Gambier, crown stays.	September	: 509 stored 27/9/60
		November	: 530 stored 7/11/60
April	: 736 stored from 22/4/60	December	: F251 stored 21/12/60

Engines condemned during 1960

The following engines were condemned during 1960, and many soon after ran their last short trip to Islington for cutting up. A few engines were also cut up by local scrap merchants.

April   : from 14/4/60: F173, F183, F237, F246, S17, S26, S136, 704, 721, 722, 724, 726, 735, 736

May   : 606, 608

A consideration in locomotive requirement levels at this stage would be the introduction of the first ten Goodwin-Alco '830' class diesels from December 1959 to June 1960, replacing engines at both Mile End and Tailem Bend sheds.

Mile End engine strength

An assessment was made in September 1960 of the engines allocated to Mile End depot, and their status. With exactly seven years of broad gauge steam operation remaining, it is interesting to look at the situation on 6/9/60:

Rx class	38 engines operational	(2 at Tailem Bend).
2nd F class	19 " "	(2 shunting Islington).
500 class	3 " "	, 2 stored, 1 parked.

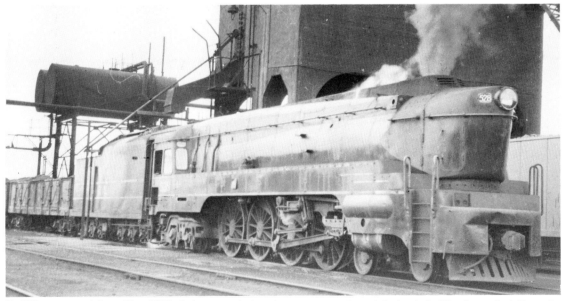

No.528 was stored from May 1960. A few years before, however, several gondolas loaded with ash required disposal, so No.528 is shown here having its coal bunker topped up, and has been assigned the task of spotting the cars in readiness for the yard engine. The dent in the streamlining above the cow-catcher explains why the sheathing was later removed from the '520' class giving them a somewhat naked front-end appearance, exaggerated by the twin sealed-beam headlights.
Photo: J.G. Southwell

520 class   5 engines operational, 3 stored, 2 parked, 2 at Islington.
620 class   1   ″   ″   , 6 parked, 1 stored, 1 at Tailem Bend.
700/710
  class   7   ″   ″   , 5 parked, 3 stored.
720 class   Nil.
740 class   10 engines operational.
750 class   1   ″   ″   , 1 parked, 6 stored, 1 repairs.

Country depots

Besides the regional depot at Tailem Bend, a number of northern centres regularly received allocation of engines from Mile End's roundhouse. The majority of these allocations were Rx class 4-6-0 locomotives, retained primarily for shunting. During the survey period of 1957-67, Terowie was the northernmost terminus of the broad gauge, an extension to Peterborough did not eventuate until after the end of steam. Below are listed country depot allocations during 1960 to 1964.

Gawler
Rx191   (March 1962)
Rx194   (April 1962)
Rx192   (June 1962)

Gladstone
Rx200   (April 1960)
Rx199   (December 1960-January 1961)
Rx231   (June 1961)
749   (July 1961)
Rx224   (January-April 1962)
Rx210   (January-September 2nd, 1963)
Rx209   (September-October 1963)
Rx210   (October 28th-end of 1964)
Rx209   (November 6th-December 1964)

Port Pirie
740   (June 1960)
Rx198   (July 1960)
Rx212   (January-August 1961)
746   (January 1961)
742   (April-June 23rd, 1961)
745   (April-November, 1961)
746   (April 1961)
719   (June-August 1961)
746   (August 1961)
742   (October-November 1st, 1961)
746   (November 1961)
746   (January-April 1962)
747   (June-December 1962)
Rx193   (September/November 1962)
748   (January-June 1963)
749   (September 1963)
Rx207   (March 15th-May 1964)
718   (September 25th-October 10th)

Snowtown
Rx232   (January-April 1960)
Rx5   (December 1960)

Rx232   (December-January 1961)
Rx229   (September 25th-December 1961)
Rx212   (November-December 1961)
Rx212   (March-September 3rd 1963)
Rx224   (October-November 1963)
Rx229   (December 17th-January 22nd, 1964)
Rx198   (January-February 1964)
Rx209   (March 9th-April 21st, 1964)
Rx225   (June 1964)
Rx224   (June 29th-July 13th, 1964)
Rx158   (July-August 1964)

Terowie
Rx225   (January-May 1960)
Rx93   (December & early January 1961)
Rx198   (December-July 1st, 1961)
Rx202   (December-January 1961)
Rx202   (July 1961)
Rx200   (July-October 1961)
Rx194   (January-February 1962)
Rx190   (March 1962)
Rx233   (November 6th-January 23rd, 1963)
Rx232   (during 1963-February 1964)
Rx200   (January-May 1963)
Rx233   (July-October 1963)
Rx225   (December 11th-April 1st, 1964)
Rx198   (March 23rd-July 21st, 1964)
Rx232   (April 20th-October 8th, 1964)
Rx200   (November-December 1964)
Rx233   (November 18th-December, 1964)

Wallaroo
Rx200   (December 24th-January 1961)
Rx210   (May 31st-August 1961)
Rx209   (August 16th-November 7th, 1961)
Rx193   (December 1961)
Rx190   (January 1962)
Rx231   (January 21st-March 19th, 1962)
Rx230   (March-May, 1962)

Wallaroo (cont.)

Rx233	(June 19th - August 19th, 1962)	Rx212	(May 1964)
Rx190	(August - September 1962)	Rx225	(August 1964)
Rx229	(December - February 10th, 1963)	Rx212	(August 1964)
Rx209	(January - March 1963)	Rx225	(September 1964)
Rx222	(March 29th - May 24th, 1963)	Rx231	(November 10th - December 15th, 1964)
Rx215	(six days in May 1963)		
Rx200	(August 28th - October 1963)		
Rx197	(January - February 6th, 1964)		
Rx228	(January 24th - 28th, 1964)		
Rx233	(February 24th - March 25th, 1964)		
Rx225	(April 1964)		

NOTE: The Power Clerk changed over engines at a predetermined elapse of time. Usually the Gladstone engine was prepared for hauling, and the Wallaroo engine was worked as a light engine both ways.

Cutting-up

The following engines were cut up by Sims, the scrap metal merchant, during 1960, and through the following year: 720, 723, 727, 728, 729, 730, 731, 732, 733 and 734.

INCIDENTS AND ACCIDENTS

Daily life at a large engine-shed, with locomotives travelling hundreds of miles a week, meant occurrences where engines would breakdown through mere wear and tear, despite rigorous maintenance. A fairly prevalent malady would be the fracture of one of the engine's cylinders, repairs that could only be carried out at the workshops. F168 found itself at Islington works in January 1960 with a right hand fracture, with Rx222 there in November for the same ailment. Another F tank No.172 was in the works again in February 1961 with a left hand cylinder fracture, and an Rx, No.140, was at Islington on 28th March 1963 with a cylinder fracture, not being returned to traffic until early May. Often cylinder repairs were only a temporary measure and Rx222 entered Islington for a new right hand cylinder in August 1964.

Fractured steam chests and 'hot boxes' (overheated axleboxes) were also inconveniences that put locomotives out of traffic for periods of time. 522 *Malcolm McIntosh* entered Islington in June 1961 with the former problem, with Rx139 also suffering a fractured chest that resulted in the engine's withdrawal soon after. Another Rx, No.218, was wheelless in October 1961 while they, and the axleboxes, were sent to the works for attention.

Collisions were unusual if not interesting events, and thankfully not too often at the expense of human

Whoops! On a sunny morning in 1950 light Pacific No.624 was easing out of Mile End loco depot when her tender derailed, disrupting movements through the lead tracks for an hour or two. The re-railing crew has not yet set to work.
Photo: J.G. Southwell

life. Rx197 entered Islington late in March 1960 after colliding, and another Rx, No.211, almost one year later for the same repairs. Mikado No.742 had to return from Port Pirie after it became derailed and received damage there in November 1961, and two years later Rx48 spent 10 days at the works, also for collision repairs. A month earlier F240 had also come into Islington with damage through collision. The same locomotive collided with Rx9 in Adelaide yard in February of the following year, and as if to challenge the authority of the new era of motive power Rx9 and Rx160 took on diesels Nos.903 and 933 later in February. Rx160 seemed to come off best in the incident, receiving only superficial damage. Finally just to prove fire can be hazardous, even to steam locomotives, 524 *Sir Mellis Napier* entered Islington in April 1964 for a repaint. The reason? It had caught alight!

1961

With the introduction of a further 7 '930' class diesels to the already operating 20, together with the previous year's introduction of 9 '830' class diesels, rationalisation of South Australian Railways broad gauge steam fleet could continue. The following engines were condemned in July 1961:

F176, F177, F184, F188, F189, F245, 502 *John Gunn*, 509 *W.A. Webb*, 525 *Sir Willoughby Norrie*, 527 *C.B. Anderson*, 528, 603, 620 *Sir Winston Dugan*, 705, 712, 751.

At the same time further reductions were made in steam strength by the decision to store or 'park' the below engines:

February
F172 (fractured cylinder a reason)
April
505 *Sir Tom Bridges*
July
508 *Sir Lancelot Stirling*
710 *Sir Alexander Ruthven*

August
716
September
744
October
743
November
F168, F174, F181, F185, F249 (boiler to the Railway's Laundry as a spare), 529 (whose tender went to No.526).

S131 at Naracoorte shortly before being condemned. This engine was specially painted for the 1954 railway's centenary, and was one of four 'S' class engines to be condemned in 1959.   Photo: S.A. Archives

Annual mileages 1961

Rx5	8440	F171	8025	Rx195	10535	Rx218	8855
Rx9	7335	F172	930	Rx197	9630	Rx222	8685
Rx15	9485	F174	320	Rx198	9445	Rx224	5820
Rx25	5090	F179	5685	Rx199	7940	Rx225	6355
Rx48	7165	F180	2010	Rx200	8555	Rx228	11670
Rx93	6715	F181	5110	Rx202	10775	Rx229	4205
Rx140	12765	F185	6710	Rx207	10755	Rx230	10530
Rx146	7010	Rx190	10300	Rx209	5850	Rx231	5225
Rx158	8130	Rx191	7245	Rx210	7155	Rx232	6190
Rx160	9020	Rx192	8595	Rx211	9930	Rx233	3370
F168	7190	Rx193	6760	Rx212	3050	F236	4265
F170	6500	Rx194	9165	Rx215	11825	F240	3640
F249	3155	523	17820	702	9475	740	8750
F250	3875	524	17310	706	5615	741	10825
F255	3910	526	18640	708	5465	742	8770
500	7995	621	4675	709	10535	743	10100
504	7440	625	855	710	6470	744	10310
505	2615	627	465	711	9850	745	12030
508	9215	628	3270	713	8244	746	14280
521	14360	700	9430	714	11735	747	10435
522	15895	701	6080	716	8335	748	8455
				717	7280	749	7155
				718	8020	752	11695
				719	12365		

The broad gauge mileages of S.A.R. steam engines were usually rounded off to the nearest five miles, but the mileage of loco No.713 specifically contains one trip with the odd end digit of four miles.

Farewell for the '500' class

With the imminent end of the '500' class in active service, the Australian Railway Historical Society in South Australia ran a trip to Murray Bridge with coal-burning No.504 *Tom Barr Smith* on October 15, 1961. It was not every day that the end of an era occurred, and so perhaps fittingly the *Advertiser* ran a sizeable article on page two of its October 16 edition headed "504 Bows out in a billow of steam".

South Australia would not see the likes of the big engines again and the tunnels and cuttings of the Adelaide Hills would certainly have 'echoed to the passage of a 500 class'. It was 504's last day in service and she took 2 hours 28 minutes to reach the Bridge (although that did include 18 minutes for photographs). The newspaper compared this pace with that of diesels which could do the trip in 85 minutes.

In charge of 504 were Lance Bewley and Ron Hale of Mile End, and both men must have had some time to ponder the '500s' passing from the stretch of line that they had been specifically designed to work, almost forty years before. And perhaps Lance Bewley summed it up for all engine crews when he told the reporter: "Diesels are easier, but there's something about a [steam] loco."

504 was put into store immediately after the trip, and so left only oil-burner 500 *James McGuire* trafficable, though it would be little more than a year before it too was placed in store. Unlike 504 (which had been earmarked for the Mile End Railway Museum) 500 would not evade the scrapper's torch.

THE LAST OF THE 'S' CLASS

The last of S.A.R.'s 4-4-0s were dispensed with during 1961, despite efforts to have one preserved for posterity. S11 had been used in 1957 as a yard shunter at Mile End, but their final stamping ground was in the South-East of the state, and apart from stored 'S' class at the closed Port Adelaide shed, Tailem Bend boasted four stored engines (S14, 17, 26 and 136) by 1959. On November 11, 1960 these four locos together with S131 and S134 entered Islington to be cut up. Despite moves to have one 'S' preserved on the foreshore at Victor Harbor, negotiations came to nothing, and the last two engines, S26 and S134, were cut up on September 8 and 21, 1961.

Other engines of note to be cut up during 1961 included: 501 in March, 525 in August, 600 September, 601 June, 602 April, 603 November, 604 July, 605 July, 607 March, 608 May, 721 February.

S128 and a Dolly at Port Adelaide in the mid-1950s. S128 was eventually condemned in 1959, and together with other 'S', 'Rx' and 'F' class engines was stored pending cutting at Port Adelaide depot. Photo: S.A. Archives

1962

Further reductions in the broad gauge steam fleet were effected in 1962, when a further 7 '830' class and 1 '930' class diesels were put into traffic. Introduction of railcars, already well under way, had already ousted most duties formerly carried out by 2nd F tanks and Rx locomotives.

Engines condemned in July 1962 included five members of the huge '500', leaving the classleader No.500 the sole operating locomotive. The by now little used '750' class Mikados were also trimmed.

Condemned July 1962: F174   F249   F251   503 *R.L. Butler*   504 *Tom Barr Smith*
505 *Sir Tom Bridges*   506 *Sir George Murray*   508 *Sir Lancelot Stirling*
530   531   715   750   753   754   756   757   758

Of a number of events that occurred in 1962, F179 was placed in store as of April 8, and Mikado No.746 (which was stored as of May 2) had its blow-off muffler transferred to No.747 to enable that loco to work at Port Pirie. Sister engine No.745, incidentally, had been stored from January 18, 1962. Pacific No.621 was involved in a trip to Moonta between May 5-6, on account of the ARHS on their "Steam Medley in Maytime" tour, while in August another 'F' was stored (No.250) following a decision made in November 1961, that the engine should be stored as soon as it became due for a 'C' or 'D' service or boiler inspection test.

Annual mileages 1962

Below are the annual (total) mileages for broad gauge engines during 1962. Unfortunately records for some of the engines on the books were unavailable. Tailem Bend engines are not included in the list.

Engine	Mileage	Engine	Mileage	Engine	Mileage	Engine	Mileage
Rx5	4545	Rx199	8730	Rx230	5315	700	1190
Rx9	4115	Rx200	3810	Rx231	5560	701	990
Rx160	8355	Rx202	7760	Rx232	2600	702	3775
F170	5125	Rx207	10590	Rx233	6940	706	4645
F171	6705	Rx209	11013	F236	3190	708	3900
F179	2210	Rx210	6295	F240	3615	746	4060
F180	Isl.	Rx211	6315	F250	3340	747	11840
Rx190	6010	Rx212	3870	F253	5245		
Rx191	7155	Rx215	8340	F255	5375		
Rx192	7095	Rx218	10005	521	15400		
Rx193	3370	Rx222	8730	522	21460		
Rx194	4920	Rx224	2800	523	14810		
Rx195	8290	Rx225	6970	526	15765		
Rx197	10280	Rx228	6330	627	3915		
Rx198	7170	Rx229	5930	628	1005		

Scrapping

Scrapping of some engines that had been out of service for a while continued during 1962. The following locos being disposed of:

No.	Month	No.	Month	No.	Month	No.	Month
502	August	609	March	712	October	735	May
506	July	703	June	715	November	736	June
507	September	704	July	722	February	750	December
508	November	705	August	724	April		
509	October	707	August	726	May		

1963

Possibly the saddest departure from the broad gauge scene in 1963 was that of the mighty 500 class 4-8-4s. After a short 'retirement' at Mile End roundhouse, No.500 *James McGuire*, by now the only serviceable member of the class, ran to Nairne in February on the pyrites freight. This duty was one of the last regular tasks of this class during the early 60s, and required tender first working Bridgewater to Nairne. To signal the end of the class the A.R.H.S. ran a series of farewell tours during March to May to Victor Harbor, Tailem Bend and Angaston, on March 17, April 28 and May 11.

Another special working around the suburbs during March was that of F170 and two carriages on what was expected to be the last steam train to Semaphore. Another special was run, for the benefit of Victorian enthusiasts, on the Port Stanvac branch. The first steam train to visit the terminal.

The closure of the Balhannah to Mount Pleasant line (opened September 16, 1918) on March 4, 1963 was recorded with special farewell trips on February 2 and March 3. Used heavily in earlier times for military specials to Woodside and Oakbank Race trains, as many as 19 trains had been scheduled on Easter Monday holidays. Engines used on these trains were mainly Mikados and '720' classes, but '500' and '520' classes were not unknown on these heavy trains. By Easter 1960 only one steam-hauled special was turned out, a legacy of the increased use of the family car, as the race meeting was no less popular. Rx199 together with three centenary cars was used on the A.R.H.S. special farewell in February 1963, while Mikado No.706 was used for the final fling on March 3. Originally No.717 was intended for the last train, and indeed was cleaned up for the occasion. However, No.706 was used due to the hot weather, having the convenience of oil-firing as against coal, and of course no likelihood of live cinders starting fires.

Also in March the last remaining loco at Naracoorte, Rx217, hauled the wayside goods to Mount Gambier where it was stabled. Mount Gambier itself finished with steam later in the month (as far as South Australian Railways was concerned) and Rx217 was sent back to Naracoorte where it remained until 1965, being the last steam loco regularly assigned to the south-east district.

At the end of May, F251 was officially presented to the South Australian Housing Trust for exhibition at Elizabeth West. When condemned in July 1962, F251 had clocked up some 877,000 miles. The choice of the tank engine for display determined the fate of an Rx engine, as No. 216 had been retained for display at Elizabeth Shopping Centre. The 'F' at Elizabeth West seemed the preferable option.

On the operating side, 526 *Duchess of Gloucester* came to grief on October 12 when it dropped a plug while returning from Port Pirie at Bowmans. Diesel No.939, working a Gladstone goods, aided 526 as far as Two Wells, where the steam engine had to be taken off, this time because it had developed a hot box. Damage to the engine was only minor, however, as it was put back into service after a few days.

During October and November 1963 the amount of steam passenger workings out of Adelaide proved to be quite considerable. The below list shows some of the rosters for big power during the period.

October 22	522 (0800 hrs Port Pirie)	November 6	522 (0800 hrs Port Pirie)
	521 (1620 hrs Tailem Bend)		524 (1230 hrs Port Pirie)
October 23	522 (0800 hrs Port Pirie)		621 (1620 hrs Tailem Bend)
	521 (1620 hrs Tailem Bend)		625 (1721 hrs Eudunda)
	524 (1852 hrs Port Pirie)		526 (1852 hrs Port Pirie)
October 24	523 (0800 hrs Port Pirie)	November 7	708 (0708 hrs Penfield & Elizabeth)
	521 (1620 hrs Tailem Bend)		522 (1800 hrs Port Pirie)
	621 (1750 hrs North Gawler)		523 (1230 hrs Port Pirie)
	526 (1852 hrs Port Pirie)		621 (1620 hrs Tailem Bend)
October 25	526 (1800 hrs Port Pirie)		625 (1721 hrs Eudunda)
October 26	747 (0710 hrs Tailem Bend)	November 8	521 (0800 hrs Port Pirie)
October 29	523 (1620 hrs Tailem Bend)		522 (1810 hrs Terowie)
	621 (1721 hrs Eudunda)	November 11	521 (1620 hrs Tailem Bend)
	521 (1750 hrs North Gawler)	November 12	526 (0800 hrs Port Pirie)
October 30	523 (1620 hrs Tailem Bend)		523 (1230 hrs Port Pirie)
	526 (1852 hrs Port Pirie)		708 (1620 hrs Tailem Bend)
October 31	700 (0708 hrs Penfield & Elizabeth)		625 (1721 hrs Eudunda)
	522 (0800 hrs Port Pirie)		524 (1810 hrs Terowie)
	621 (1721 hrs Eudunda)	November 13	522 (0800 hrs Port Pirie)
November 1	523 (0800 hrs Port Pirie)		625 (1620 hrs Tailem Bend)
November 5	522 (0800 hrs Port Pirie)		523 (1852 hrs Port Pirie)
	526 (1620 hrs Tailem Bend)		F255* (2010 hrs Belair)
	Rx140 (1721 hrs Eudunda)	November 14	625 (1620 hrs Tailem Bend)
	524 (1810 hrs Terowie)		621 (1721 hrs Eudunda)
			523 (1810 hrs Terowie)

* The use of F255 on a Belair train was a special excursion by A.R.H.S. members, and it was the first time an 'F' had been to Belair since November 1959.

The seasonal Myer Santa specials in November 1963 saw 'light' Mikado No.752 in charge of trains to Marino (November 18), North Gawler (19th), Bridgewater (20th), Outer Harbor (21st) and North Gawler (22nd).

Workshop visitors in 1963
The following locomotives visited Islington during 1963 for the specified services. By now Mile End only carried out 'A' services, many of its service staff having been transferred to Islington at the end of 1962. Dates, where specified, are the 'outshop' dates after the specified service.

January	713('C'), Rx212	August	Rx215 (ex-'B' 3/9/63)
February	713 (ex-'C' 6/3/64)		F255 (ex-'D' 13/9/63)
	522 (ex-'D' 15/2/63)		523 (ex-'D' 3/9/63)
	701 (ex-'B' 22/3/63)		526 (ex-'D' 30/9/63)
March	Rx140 (cylinder fracture)		700 (removal of oil burner)
	718 ('B'), 747 (ex-'B' 24/4/63)	September	700 (coal burner from 6/9/63)
	708 (ex-'C' 11/4/63)		706 (removal of oil burner)
April	F171, Rx231 (ex-'C' 27/5/63)	October	Rx199 (ex-'D' 16/10/63)
	718 (ex-'B' 8/5/63)		Rx225 (ex-'D' 7/11/63)
	625 (ex-'B' 29/5/63), Rx140		706 (coal burner from 29/10/63)
May	752 (ex-'B' 7/6/63)	November	Rx48 (10 days; collision repair)
	F170 (to works, then shunt)		Rx229 (ex-'B' 14/11/63)
	Rx233 (ex-'D' 7/6/63)		F236 (ex-'C' 11/12/63)
	Rx140 (ex-cylinder repair 8/5/63)		F240 (ex-'B' 29/11/63)
June	Rx222 (special repairs)		627 (ex-'B' 18/11/63)
	Rx230 (ex-'C' 10/7/63)	December	Rx9, 522 (ex-'B' 24/2/63)
	524 (ex-'D' 26/7/63)		
July	Rx5, Rx209 (ex-'C' 26/7/63)		
	Rx218 (ex-'C' 5/8/63)		
	Rx222 (ex-special repairs)		

Comings and goings

Further rationalisation of power requirements on the broad gauge system saw a number of movements by the surviving steam fleet. In January 1963, Mikado No.748 was sent to Port Pirie for shunting duties, and it remained there until June. Rx25 was stored at Mile End on February 8 on account of a fractured steam chest, its tender was exchanged with that being used by operational Rx231.

Mikado No.745 last worked in December 1961, and was stored from January 18, 1962.   Photo: G. Bishop

Spick-and-span Mikado No.717 sits alone on the ready track at Mile End in March 1963.   Photo: J.G. Southwell

Pacific No.623 was sent to Tailem Bend, in conjunction with the Queen's visit, on February 8 and was to work for the final time on March 20, being stored from April 11. As an indication of mileages being covered by some members of this class, 623 covered 33,375 miles between a 'D' service on May 2, 1958 and September 13, 1961.

To cover the Pacific's imminent withdrawal, No.628 of Mile End was transferred to Tailem Bend from March 1963. Three Rx locos were stored during March when Rx55 was sent back from Tailem Bend on March 22 (having last worked on December 11, 1962). Also on March 22, Rx139 was put into storage, with its splashers and sandboxes being sent to Islington, plus its fractured steam chest. The storage was only preceding eventual cutting up. The engine had covered a mere 1584 miles since its last overhaul. Rx216 which had been put into storage at Tailem Bend from March 6, was sent to Mile End for storage on March 22.

F180, which was at Islington during all of 1963, replaced F253 as a works shunter while the latter was receiving a service from March 6. The outshopping of Pacific No.625 from Islington on May 29 didn't improve the frequency with which some members of this class were utilised. 625 worked only 27 days during 1963, a small total indeed. Yet in 1961 it only worked a total of eight days!

Another Islington works shunter during the first half of 1963 was F244 which finished its term of service there on June 21, having been allocated to the works on May 30 of the previous year.

Later allocations to Port Pirie during the latter half of 1963 included 749 in September, and 718 between September 25 and October 10.

Cutting up
The following engines, some of which had been condemned for a while, were cut up during 1963. Although not a comprehensive list, it does include most larger power engines eliminated.

503 (16/2/63 at Islington), 505 (29/4/63 at Islington), 527 (24/5/63 at Islington), 528 (21/6/63 at Islington), 530 (24/9/63 at Islington), 531 (13/8/63 at Islington), 606 (the last member of the class 28/2/63 at Islington), 620 (5/7/63 at Islington), 740 (8/11/63 at Islington), 743 (December 1963 at Islington), 748 (8/11/63 at Islington), 751 (1/2/63 at Islington), 753 (19/2/63), 754 (13/3/63 at Islington), 756 (3/5/63 at Islington), 757 (29/5/63 at Islington) and 758 (18/6/63 at Islington).

Annual mileages 1963

Rx5	5825	Rx210	4340	Rx232	9690	700	1645
Rx9	5105	Rx211	10295	Rx233	7505	701	2685
Rx25	330*	Rx212	4350	F236	5325	702	8830
Rx48	8000	Rx215	8615	F240	5095	706	4110
Rx55	1020†	Rx218	8590	F244	3460	708	3260
Rx93	7325	Rx222	5765	F253	5350	709	8115
F170	1865‡	Rx224	5195	521	17110	713	5065
F171	6215	Rx225	6890	522	17555	714	3630
F180	Islington	Rx228	9510	523	17430	717	7445
Rx200	10700	Rx229	5865	524	17755	718	4695
Rx207	2520	Rx230	7450	526	18025	747	12185
Rx209	7435	Rx231	5470	623	830§	748	9840
				625	2935	749	11495
				628	1985‡	752	1780

NOTES:
* Engine stored February 8, account of fractured steam chest.
† Engine returned from Tailem Bend March 22, having last worked on December 11, 1962. Stored from July 3, 1963.
✦ Engine to Islington for shunting from May 1963. Still there at December 31, 1964.
§ Engine stored from April 11.
‡ Engine transferred to Tailem Bend records from March. (A number of records for Rx class engines were not available for the year 1963.)

Rx25 had been stored from February 1963 because of a fractured steam chest. Its six-wheel self-trimming tender had latterly been used by Rx231. The tender on the flat wagon was eventually destined for the Mile End Railway Museum.
Photo: J. Wilson

In 1963 the only additions to the diesel fleet was the introduction of 18 '830' class diesels, most destined for the narrow gauge. Despite this, further reductions were made in the steam fleet with the final withdrawal of the mighty '500' class 4-8-4s, No.500 itself. The Rx class began to have further members withdrawn from service after a number of years free of eliminations. More important though was the withdrawal of members of the '740' class, with the exception of a few locomotives which saw service shunting at Port Pirie.

Engines condemned in 1963:

May   500 *James McGuire*
October Rx191, Rx216

July   F168, F181, F185, F241, 529,
710 *Sir Alexander Ruthven*, 711, 719, 740, 741, 742, 743, 745, 746, 748, 759.

1964

By 1964 many of the broad gauge steam classes were working only a small percentage of the monthly mileages they had in 1960. The Rx class locomotives were enjoying an 'Indian summer' in their new role as shunters, and would last a little longer until the introduction of the red '500' class diesels was under way. As useful as ever was the '520' class 'light' 4-8-4s, whose surviving members still managed to work passenger expresses, including the Port Pirie service.

Annual mileages 1964

Engine No.	Jan	Feb	March	April	May	June	July	August	Sept	Oct	Nov	Dec	TOTAL
Rx5	405	560	420	415	430	680	680	730	300	...stored 28/10/64			4620
Rx9	*	270	470	690	405	245	50	370	—	560	370	430	3860
Rx15	—	170	810	475	1175	630	390	255	165	295	50	330	4745
Rx48	445	590	715	690	140	450	610	260	350	1230	1010	395	6885
Rx93	—	1395	1280	990	935	440	750	1550	1405	1320	700	550	11315
Rx140	845	755	700	425	490	940	890	395	415	590	350	375	7170
Rx146	845	550	520	200	—	825	850	410	345	500	780	940	6765
Rx158	1005	825	855	1195	620	580	585	315	610	250	470	570	7880
Rx160	410	110	*	430	250	305	200	490	375	430	370	260	3630
F171	440	530	900	510	60	*	*	180	430	270	280	250	3850
Rx190	190	610	400	365	105	545	670	425	615	440	770	270	5405
Rx192	535	40	1095	1010	775	1435	350	530	560	470	530	855	8185
Rx193	535	510	90	360	1110	*	120	—	400	680	430	810	5045
Rx194	1170	240	710	640	650	885	1200	360	340	230	130	120	6675
Rx195	870	770	1070	800	835	880	385	200	990	920	700	555	8975
Rx197	1080	595	350	1105	795	715	725	850	640	230	790	490	8365
Rx198	180	*	410	1320	1860	1330	1150	555	385	360	240	420	8210
Rx199	930	525	525	410	800	470	925	680	935	970	240	400	7810
Rx200	835	460	730	945	955	955	350	430	545	70	590	940	7805
Rx202	290	370	650	745	110	500	795	380	685	360	360	—	5245
Rx207	—	—	—	—	530	800	170	840	640	640	700	140	4460
Rx209	310	530	210	80	780	365	770	500	180	145	380	210	4460
Rx210	270	470	395	385	415	75	295	—	285	20	—	130	2740
Rx211	*	370	695	1225	710	1085	955	405	710	530	510	285	7480
Rx212	345	385	755	160	615	725	875	720	—	320	325	330	5555
Rx215	840	665	935	965	740	740	795	1155	580	190	270	850	8725
Rx218	505	805	1075	875	970	910	845	535	520	620	900	1065	9625
Rx222	225	555	735	945	770	40	*	360	*	500	900	480	5510
Rx224	715	580	380	420	960	705	285	915	410	830	40	715	6955
Rx225	1400	1680	1310	980	895	300	620	880	505	650	640	150	10010
Rx228	790	760	720	645	640	660	225	530	750	670	1040	770	8200
Rx229	—	675	830	530	1030	290	515	755	360	650	690	330	6655
Rx230	960	960	825	380	685	470	600	*	290	720	1220	835	7945
Rx231	205	485	150	*	830	870	810	245	425	30	80	130	4260

Engine No.	Jan	Feb	March	April	May	June	July	August	Sept	Oct	Nov	Dec	TOTAL
Rx232	830	570	420	940	1370	880	1055	1575	1090	750	400	480	10360
Rx233	590	640	1070	350	990	190	150	280	670	490	990	1245	7655
F236	740	440	480	760	525	510	590	400	255	440	550	355	6045
F240	580	150	190	280	250	430	230	100	160	500	140	615	3625
F244	650	380	910	560	500	410	270	*	240	240	270	480	4910
F253	310	440	—	—	250	210	220	335	585	330	370	180	3230
F255	300	720	520	510	310	350	165	240	165	150	190	190	3810
520	—	—	—	—	1320	1745	2400	2030	3060	315	1090	2595	14555
521	1050	1145	*	1805	1545	1420	1235	1235	2170	1235	1775	1370	15985
522	*	160	3065	2670	1120	1765	360	2085	1820	1620	1460	2485	18610
523	1520	2320	1825	400	1665	*	1570	—	1400	1745	350	1140	13935
524	—	*	1845	1690	2250	1495	980	855	1925	1995	1765	1770	16570
526	2755	2220	2480	3040	2595	1355	1590	1720	*	695	1695	2700	22845
621	375	235	350	440	—	—	—	—	—	—	—	—	1400
625	—	—	305	305	80	—	—	—	210	305	200	420	1825
627	—	705	690	1010	—	—	—	445	285	—	—	155	3290
700	330	680	—	475	580	640	400	580	745	650	1050	*	6130
701	110	485	270	335	220	*	—	—	280	50	305	555	2610
702	—	—	stored 26/3/64 ...										—
706	450	360	195	205	670	—	—	700	800	770	—	70	4220
708	—	500	560	620	550	250	350	110	*	100	300	330	3670
709	—	*	595	470	805	310	890	80	1105	740	480	870	6345
713	820	790	1340	300	140	... stored from 14/5/64							3390
717	—	250	1185	665	—	1415	1050	480	80	585	800	480	6990
718	1160	680	435	1190	—	460	790	530	*	*	800	880	6925
747	840	440	450	580	885	810	140	... stored 7/7/64					4145
752	530	290	100	570	*	—	—	—	—	420	470	200	2580

* Signifies at works.

'740' class Mikado No.748 accelerates north from Mile End with a freight bound for Port Pirie in the 1960s.
Photo: J.G. Southwell

Tailem Bend

This depot still retained a small allocation of engines in 1964 for shunting and the occasional branch working. Engines listed as being allocated to this depot, although some were at this stage in effect stored, were: Rx20, Rx56, Rx155, Rx201, Rx208, Rx217, Rx219, Rx227, Rx235, 628, 755.

Scrapping

During 1964 a number of locomotives that had been condemned for a while were at last sent to Islington for cutting-up. Included were the following:

January	F241	**July**	741, 745
February	F181, 746	**August**	744, 749, 623, 759, F179, F250
April	F168, F185	**October**	719
June	742	**November**	714
		December	500

The return to traffic of 520 *Sir Malcolm Barclay-Harvey* on May 7 was brought about by a serious power shortage out of Mile End roundhouse. It began with a short test trip to Gawler, and totalled over a thousand miles in the first month's service. The return of 520 followed the fire damage of 523 *Essington Lewis* at the roundhouse on April 15. A flare-up in the cab caused scarring of paintwork. 523 re-entered traffic early in May following a repaint at Islington.

Among the departures from Mile End in 1964, was that of Rx191 which left in the consist of No.955 Victor Harbor goods on June 17. The engine was despatched to be put on permanent display on the Harbor foreshore. Although it remains a fitting reminder to the class that served the line for many years, it is nonetheless a poor substitute for the now extinct 'S' class loco that was originally negotiated for display in the town.

Another Rx engine was taking part in history during July, when Rx158 brought the last regular Truro goods in from Gawler. Rx228 had originally set off with the train but had run 'hot' at Gawler and had to be replaced. The following month another engine, Rx5, became the last steam engine to work the weekly Bumbunga-Lochiel goods on August 24. The engine had been stabled at Snowtown 'depot' at the time.

The nearby railway museum at Mile End received its first exhibit in August also, when P117 was pushed into the site by Rx200. The 'P', which was the last surviving example of its type, had been withdrawn from Tailem Bend in late December 1956. Since withdrawal it had spent some time stored at Stewarts and Lloyd, Kilburn, until moved from there by another Rx (215).

October 1 saw the return to traffic of the 'last of the '750' class, No.752. The engine had been waiting on plugs for several months and during its running-in period worked the Glanville goods on October 1, 2, 6, 7 and 8. A visitor to Mile End roundhouse during the month was Rx235 up from Tailem Bend for light repairs.

November saw another Tailem Bend engine, Rx214, also at Mile End for light repairs on November 7. Three days later an 'F' class briefly returned to passenger duty when F244 worked the Islington workman's train. This train at the time was usually loco hauled, power being provided by either '930', '830' or '800' class diesels. On rare occasions an 'Rx' was rostered.

Steam retained turns

During the early to mid 1960s, the number of steam turns did not decrease as quickly as anticipated, and though diesels would be used in preference to steam, if available, some turns still saw steam in charge when power shortages occurred. Below are listed some of the turns that saw the substitution of steam for diesel from time to time.

0030 hrs   Tailem Bend 'scavenger' which was sometimes powered by a '700' class Mikado. The service was so called as it stopped frequently to drop and pick up wagons.

0611 hrs	On Tuesday this service to Truro was usually a duty for the surviving '750' Mikado, No.752 — when it was trafficable.
0800 hrs	Port Pirie passenger service, when a diesel was unavailable, and was worked by a '520' up until late 1966.
1620 hrs	Tailem Bend passenger Monday to Thursday, which was usually in the charge of a '520' or '620' class engine.
1630 hrs	Willunga (on Tuesday) which was frequented by a Mikado, but in fact could have anything at its head.
1852 hrs	Port Pirie (Wednesday) passenger, which again was a '520' turn.

Besides the usual shunting duties, an Rx class engine would work to Wallaroo once a week, and the Wednesday night extra Port Pirie goods still employed steam at its head. Mikados No.748 and 749 saw service at Port Pirie at various spells on shunting duty, and No.747 was the final engine of its class to serve this town.

By the beginning of 1964, however, 747 was the last of its type in traffic, and to mark the demise of the class a farewell trip was organised using the engine to Bridgewater on June 27 and Eudunda on July 4.

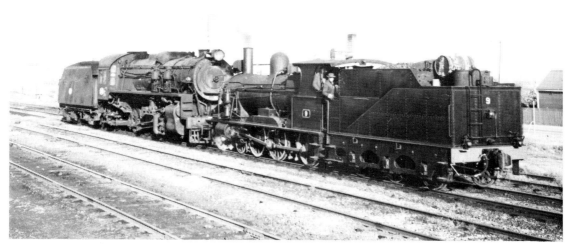

One of the first exhibits in the Mile End Railway Museum was Mikado No.702, being moved to the site by Rx9 on June 1, 1965.
Photo: J.G. Southwell

TESTING OF BOILERS

An important part of regular locomotive maintenance was the annual boiler inspection test carried out on all South Australian Railways steam engines, irrespective of whether the engines were operational or stored. The following procedures were set out in Mechanical Department Instruction sheet No. 88, entitled "Testing of Steam Boilers".

1. Hydraulic Tests Method of Applying
   Whenever possible all hydraulic tests shall be made with warm water at a temperature not exceeding 150 degrees F. and in filling boilers, care should be taken to expel all air from domes and other natural pockets.
   The pressure shall be obtained by means of an approved pump and shall be raised slowly and steadily until the standard test pressure is reached. The pressure shall be maintained for a minimum period of fifteen minutes but this period must be extended if necessary in order to permit a thorough examination of the boiler under pressure.

2. Master Gauges
   The test pressure shall be measured by means of an approved master gauge, in addition to the gauge belonging to the boiler under test. All gauges shall be fitted with stop cocks.

3. Safety valves
   During hydraulic tests safety valves shall be removed or each valve secured against lifting by means of a suitable testing clamp. Valves must not be secured by screwing down or by any other method which will over stress the springs.

4. Hammer Testing of Welded Seams
   When applying the hydraulic test to boilers with welded seams, such seams shall be hammer tested while under test pressure. A four (4) pound hammer shall be used and blows shall be struck smartly on each side of the welded seams along its full length at intervals of three (3) inches apart, and within three inches of the line of weld. To avoid injury to pressure gauges stop cocks shall be shut off during hammer testing.

5. Testing of New Locomotive Boilers
   Each new locomotive boiler after completion and before clothing is applied shall be subjected to a hydraulic test of one and one half times the maximum permissible working pressure.

6. Testing of Repaired Locomotive Boilers
   Each repaired locomotive boiler, after completion of repairs and before clothing is applied shall be subjected to a hydraulic test pressure of one and one quarter times the maximum permissible working pressure.
   This clause does not apply where less than 50% of the tubes are renewed or where minor running repairs only are made.

7. Periodical Testing of Locomotive Boilers
   Each new locomotive boiler shall be subjected to a hydraulic test pressure of one and one quarter times the maximum permissible pressure once every twelve (12) months. This test shall be made at the same time as the annual inspection and the clothing shall be wholly or partly removed only if considered necessary by the Boiler Inspector.

8. Testing of Locomotive Boilers for Stationary use
   All locomotive boilers used for stationary purpose shall have all clothing removed and be subjected to a hydraulic pressure of one and one quarter times the maximum permissible working pressure once every twelve (12) months. This test shall be made at the same time as the annual inspection.

9. Testing of New Stationary Boilers
   Each stationary boiler with rivetted joints, when new and before clothing is applied, shall be subjected to a hydraulic pressure test of twice the permissible working pressure up to one hundred (100) pounds per square inch, and one and one half times the maximum permissible working pressure over one hundred (100) pounds per square inch.

10. Testing of stationary Boilers after extensive repairs
    Each stationary boiler after receiving extensive repairs shall, before the clothing is applied, be subjected to a hydraulic test pressure of one and one half times the maximum permissible working pressure.

F240 and Rx210 bask in the afternoon winter sun at Mile End roundhouse on June 1, 1965.   Photo: J. Wilson

By early 1965 the roundhouse 'treasure' was the last of the mighty '500' class No.504 Tom Barr Smith. Although condemned for many years, it was stored at the roundhouse pending its departure to the Railway Museum a short distance from the depot. This view was taken on June 1.   Photo: J. Wilson

BOILER INSPECTION REPORTS

During the above inspection a full report of the condition of the boiler was recorded on the "Boiler Inspection Report", a blue sheet measuring some 34 x 39 cms. in size. The sheet was sectionalised into 12 parts, clearly setting out the parts of the boiler to be inspected, with remarks, assessment of condition and repairs required noted alongside. Section 41, for example, dealt with the barrel, 42 the casing and so on to 59, water gauges, pressure gauges and safety valves. Finally an overall assessment made of the boiler and authorisation was either given or declined for the engine to operate a further 12 months. An example of a tender locomotive is given below.

Gauge 5' 3"   Class RX   Engine No. 194   Boiler No. 430
                                                                                                                                                                      saturated

Age 28½ YEARS   Working pressure 175 lb. sq. in.   Inspection 6th Annual
Issued to Traffic 23/2/1956   Last Inspected 14/3/62   Date Inspected 20/9/63
mileage since last overhaul 85708 miles   Mile End Depot

Section	Detail	New or repair	Remarks, Condition and Repairs needed
41 (Barrel)	1st course		Good, seams leaking to caulk
	2nd "		Good
	3rd "		Good
	Dome		Good
42 (Casing)	Throatplate		Good, (6 flexible stay cups rewelded, 3 cups renewed)
	Wrapperplate		Good, to clean externally
	Side sheet R		Good, 9 flexible stay cups rewelded
	" L		Good, 14 flexible stay cups rewelded
	Backplate		Good, 2 flexible stay cups rewelded
	" Braces		Good
	Expansion brackets		Good
43 (Firebox)	Tubeplate		Good, to pean in fire area
	Crown sheet		Good, to clean internally
	Side sheet R		Good, to pean in fire area
	" L		Good, to pean in fire area
	Throatplate		Nil
	Door sheet		Good, to pean in fire area
	Comb chamber		Nil
	Syphons		Nil
44	Smokebox Tubeplate		Good, to chip and paint below tube area
	" Braces		Good
45 (Ring)	Foundation		Good, foundation ring rivet head to chip and paint in firebox, corner rivets to
	Firedoor		Good
	Stoker door		Nil
	Angle Iron		Good
46 (Stays)	Flexible		Good (8 ball stays renewed. Test holes to open up)
	Rigid		Good (to chip above crown sheet firebox)

Section	Detail	New or repair	Remarks, Condition and Repairs needed
	Girder		Nil
	Belly		Good
	Cross		Good
	Longitudinal		Good
	Water space		Good
47	Roof Bars		Nil
48	Tubes		Good, 150 removed a/c heavy scale
	Flues		Nil
	Arch Tubes		Nil
54	Elements		Nil
49	Smokebox		Good
	″ door		Good
(smokebox)	″ ring		Good
	″ crossbar		Good
	Chimney		Good
50	Ashpan & rigging		To overhaul
(ashpan)	Carriers		Good
	Slides & doors		Good
	Damper doors		Good
	Shaker grate		To overhaul
56	Washout plugs		Good, to clean & refit 5 renewed
	Fusible plugs		To renew
	Brick Arch studs		Good
	Stay caps removed for tests		Nil
59	Water Gauges		To overhaul, steam & waterways to clear
	Pressure gauges		To test
	Safety valves		To overhaul, checked under steam test.

Remarks:— Boiler stripped and removed from frame on account boiler repairs. It is anticipated that this boiler which is in good condition and safe to work at a steam pressure of 175 lbs. per square inch will require General Overhaul 1966.

When engines went to Islington for B.I.T. they were usually given a fresh coat of paint.

Although conducted annually, B.I.T. were later carried out at extended periods when locomotives were working infrequently. In these cases examinations were made because mileage accrued, rather than mere lapse of time.

1965

The following locomotives were recorded by the Office of the Loco Foreman as being at Mile End at 28/2/65.

Rx class 4-6-0
5 (stored), 9, 15, 25 (condemned), 48, 55 (condemned), 93, 139 (condemned), 140, 146, 158, 160, 190, 192, 193, 194, 195, 197, 198, 199, 200, 202, 207, 209, 210, 211, 212, 215, 218, 222, 224, 225, 228, 229, 230, 231, 232, 233

Total: 38

2nd F class 4-6-2T
170, 171, 180, 236, 240, 244, 253, 255

Total: 8

500 class 4-8-4
504 *Tom Barr Smith* (condemned but retained for Railway Museum)

Total: 1

520 class 4-8-4

520 *Sir Malcolm Barclay-Harvey*	523 *Essington Lewis*
521 *Thomas Playford*	524 *Sir Mellis Napier*
522 *Malcolm McIntosh*	526 *Duchess of Gloucester*

Total: 6

620 class 4-6-2
621, 622 (parked), 625, 626, (parked), 627, 629 (parked)

Total: 6

700/710 class 2-8-2
700, 701, 702 (condemned but retained for Railway Museum), 706, 708, 709, 713 (stored), 716 (condemned), 717, 718

Total: 10

740 class 2-8-2
747 (stored)

Total: 1

750 class 2-8-2
752

Total: 1

By the end of May 1965 Nos. 628, 755 and Rx227 had returned from Tailem Bend depot and had joined the above at Mile End. By early November 1965, No.621 had been stopped on account of valves and hydro, No.625 had been stopped because its Boiler Inspection Test was overdue. Mikado No.701 had been stopped on account of a fractured sidebar frame and 'light' Mikado, No.755, was officially 'parked'. Rx class, No.146 had been stopped after collision repairs became necessary, while F tanks Nos. 170 and 180 were employed at Islington as works shunters.

During 1965 a number of unusual workings marked the continuing use of steam when power shortages occurred, despite the end of steam operations being just two years away. Steam returned to the Victor Harbor line in January, when local residents requested the use of steam on the 0900 hrs train from Adelaide on January 9 and 16. 526 *Duchess of Gloucester* carried 178 passengers on the former date, with 168 passengers still on at Goolwa (train no.341). For the return 192 passengers boarded, with 172 still on after Goolwa (train no.830). On January 16, 524 *Sir Mellis Napier* took 300 passengers out of Adelaide, with 299 still on the train after Goolwa. No passenger count for the return trip is available.

Yet another 'first' in steam operation occurred relatively late in broad gauge steam operation in February 1965, when the ARHS ran the first large power locomotive (apart from the 750 class) over the Port line. Mikado No.718 on an eight-car train took the honour, working the Adelaide-Hendon and Outer Harbor routes. Although a Mikado had worked to Woodville some years before, it had reached there by way of the Finsbury loop from Gillman yard. Similarly, when some '720' class engines were sent to Port Adelaide for cutting up in the early sixties, they reached there via Dry Creek.

Locomotive movements during 1965 at Mile End roundhouse included the departure of Rx55 behind diesel No.960 and the 107-ton wrecking crane bound for Tailem Bend, and eventually Loxton for preservation. It stayed at the Bend until November 21 when it was included in the consist of the 843 mixed to Loxton. Sister Rx56 was also at Tailem Bend during this period, and by mid-1965 was per-

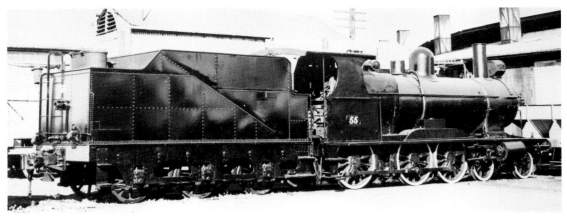

Rx55 was prepared by Tailem Bend shop forces for display at Loxton. Resplendent in fresh paint she stands behind the roundhouse, awaiting her final journey late in November 1965. Photo: J.G. Southwell

By 1965 a sizeable section of the roundhouse had been demolished, and in this May 28 view locos 713, 755, 628 and 504 are already in outside storage. Photo: D. Moyses

For a number of years the annual Myer Santa Specials were in the hands of '620' Pacifics. Here No.627 waits to take out one of the trains on November 15, 1965. Photo: J. Wilson

manently fitted for steam generation at the depot. Other engines there either stored or retained for seasonal or occasional use were: Rx155, 201, 208, 214, 217, 219, 235 and Pacific No.624, which had a firebox 'fitted' with a mattress and other items — obviously designed for a quiet kip!

Steam operations during 1965 called for Mile End engines to do a number of Tailem Bend trips. On May 26 Mikado No.717 left Mile End with the wrecking crane in tow in the consist of a mixed goods, and No.625 worked the up Tailem Bend passenger getting into Adelaide after 1130 hrs, while a '520' worked the 1620 hrs return. Pacific No.628 and Mikado No.755 were hauled back from Tailem Bend for storage at Mile End, while 717 returned with a Tailem Bend passenger on May 29.

Steam returned to the Tailem-Murray Bridge mixed from November 23 after the rostered diesel, No.504, developed bad 'flats' on its wheels, and had to be taken out of service. Rx engines were used from November 23-26 (Rx214, 219, 208 and 235) though Rx219 had to be relieved of its duty on November 24 when it dropped a plug. Rx208 was sent to the rescue. Mile End provided steam late in 1965 for the Myer Santa specials, No.627 working it on November 19.

The following engines were condemned during 1965:
June   Rx20.   **November**   Rx5, Rx233, 713, 747.

Rather ominously, Mile End roundhouse was closed from December 25 until January 4, 1966 (the Christmas period) and during that time all of the Adelaide division workings were diesel powered. While the roundhouse had been closed over Christmas, earlier in the year the small coaling stage at Riverton was demolished.

Summary of SAR broad gauge steam mileages during 1965

Engine No.	Jan	Feb	March	April	May	June	TOTAL	July-December class average
F class *	1661	1492	843	750	622	614	5982	114*
Rx class *	16960	16442	17987	13485	12694	12031	89599	266*
520	1303	1162	2134	2564	280	285	7728	596†
521	1276	869	1311	—	1624	1456	6536	
522	1337	280	113	2077	1632	1417	6856	
523	140	1766	840	1855	2551	999	8151	
524	882	2373	1609	1877	1316	1414	9471	
526	1575	1903	2119	1410	1874	714	9595	
621	—	233	1319	152	—	—	1704	152†
624	—	—	—	—	822	79	901	
625	154	—	625	154	1167	—	2100	
627	—	284	1954	760	430	—	3428	
700	4	445	284	404	691	234	2062	235†
701	329	203	437	—	—	—	969	
706	—	30	171	282	935	354	1772	
708	—	247	364	582	75	634	1902	
709	68	151	272	497	105	55	1148	
717	132	173	296	566	652	277	2096	87†
718	8	45	258	305	552	130	1298	

NOTES: *Signifies class *total* mileages during January-June 1965, and class *average* milages during July-December 1965.

†Signifies *average* class mileages during July-December 1965. Rx56 (used as stationary boiler) and Rx217 of Tailem Bend depot were sent to Islington on November 3 and August 31 respectively.

Of the F class mileages in the January-June period the following engines were used in part or all of the half year : 170, 171, 180, 236, 240, 244, 253 and 255.

In the Rx class mileages over the same half year period between 34 and 38 engines of the class were used each month. Highest individual monthly mileages were run by Rx155 (1812 January), Rx201 (1536 February), Rx214 (1355 March), Rx201 (1059 April). Rx201 (809 May) and Rx217 (2046 June).

1966

During this year there was a considerable reduction in steam rosters, which was no doubt assisted to some extent by the introduction in 1965 of eight '500' class diesels and five '930' locos. To this was added a further five '500' diesels in 1966. In June the last of the '740' class Mikados, No.747, together with no. 713 were towed to Islington for cutting up. However, this wasn't the end of these two. Their tenders were converted at the works as brake tenders for use at Tailem Bend, and they were issued to traffic on October 25.

Basically what was done — the bodies of the tenders were replaced by a block of concrete about 15 inches thick, auto couplers were fitted to both ends of the tender, and so fitted they could be coupled or detached from their '500' class diesel pairing at will.

One of the few rosters later in 1966 involved the use of 521 *Thomas Playford* on a few turns in September. It worked one of the last steam hauled Port Pirie passenger trains on September 14 (the 1852 hrs ex-Adelaide shopping train) being the first steam on the line in about two months. On September 21 it went to Tailem Bend on the 1620 hrs, ex-Adelaide, and then did an outing to Willunga, probably as part of 'running-in' after receiving a service and B.I.T. at Islington.

Country depot allocations were still being made, and in April 1966 an Rx was sent to Wallaroo with two cars and eight wheel brake, and took up spare exchange.

By September it was noted that only three or four engines were being lit up at the roundhouse on weekdays, and none at all on weekends. At this time an F class tank was usually employed shunting round the depot area. Gladstone still retained two Rx engines, and Terowie kept one. All three engines seemed to gain regular work. Rx225 returned from Wallaroo, and in so doing became the last steam locomotive in regular traffic to spend time at that depot. Tailem Bend also still had Rx allocations. However, during this period they saw little regular use. During this period tenders were called for the removal of further flung coal plants at Bordertown, Naracoorte and Mount Gambier. The one at Bordertown was noteworthy in that it straddled the main line, and so enabled engines to be coaled without leaving their train. The coaling stage at Mount Gambier had not been used by South Australian engines for quite a while, but Victorian steam locos were working into the Mount only weeks before tenders were called for the coal stage removal. It was finally pulled down in January 1967.

Summary of mileages in 1966

Engine No.	Jan	Feb	March	April	May	June	July	August	Sept	Oct	Nov	Dec	TOTAL
F class*	609	572	633	516	693	733	749	753	718	597	737	520	7830
Rx class*	4997	4174	5020	3518	5286	4261	3309	2440	2508	1963	1832	1592	40900
520	—	—	880	—	—	588	435	—	—	170	—	—	2073
521	280	280	—	552	154	—	—	139	434	47	269	—	2155
522	—	272	710	277	—	180	281	—	—	—	—	—	1720
523	565	280	154	1070	1145	991	282	—	50	—	—	—	4537
524	—	—	—	—	—	274	—	—	—	280	—	—	554
526	—	154	631	434	1330	972	34	280	—	—	—	172	4007
624	—	—	—	—	68	72	170	100	—	—	—	—	410
700	—	—	—	—	—	154	—	—	—	—	—	—	154
706	—	—	193	—	—	—	—	—	—	—	—	—	193
717	—	—	58	—	—	—	—	—	—	—	—	—	58
718	—	—	178	154	—	150	—	—	—	—	—	—	282

Rx 158 was one of the last of its class to be withdrawn from 'on the books', during February 1969. It made itself useful up to 1967 on pilot duty. It's seen at Mile End in November 1965
Photo: M. Billett

NOTES: *Signifies total mileages of all engines used in class. In the case of the Rxs, 23 worked in January, 19 in February, 20 in March, 16 April, 18 May, 17 June, 18 July, 14 August, 16 September, 11 October, 12 November, 12 December. Engines Nos. 15, 158, 160, 197, 210, 218, 225 and 228 were individual highest monthly accruers.

Of the F class locos, 6 engines worked in January, 4 February, 4 March, 3 April, 4 May, 3 June, 4 July, 4 August, 4 September, 3 October, 3 November and 4 in December. Eight serviceable engines remained during 1966 (F170, 171, 180, 236, 240, 244, 253 and 255), these being shuffled round to cover the year's duties including workshop shunting at Islington.

The mileages accrued by locos 624, 700, 717 and 718 were all the result of special trains, and would not, in all likelihood, have been used in normal traffic.

The infrequency of steam rosters from Mile End roundhouse by mid 1966 can be gauged by these sample daily rosters covering July to November 1966.

Wednesday 27/7/1966
Pilots for the day: 522 *Malcolm McIntosh*, Rx218
Rx218 (0615 hrs. Light engine Dry Creek, Smithfield, Penfield, North Adelaide).
Rx197 (0910 hrs. Shunt)
Rx158 (0602 hrs. Shunt)   Stabling times: Rx197 (1600 hrs)
Rx160 (0602 hrs. Shunt)   Rx158 (2000 hrs)
Engines receiving washouts: Rx192, Rx229, Rx232.

Monday 8/8/1966
Pilots for the day: 526 *Duchess of Gloucester*, Rx232.
Rx212 (0602 hrs. Shunt)
F255 (0700 hrs. Islington works as shunter)   Stabling times: Rx192 (1600 hrs)
Rx192 (0910 hrs. Shunt)   Rx212 (2000 hrs)

Wednesday 17/8/66
Pilots for the day: Rx 160, 526 *Duchess of Gloucester*.
Rx218 (0602 hrs. Shunt)
Rx212 (0730 hrs. Shunt)   Stabling times: Rx212 (0930 hrs)
Rx232 (0910 hrs. Shunt)   Rx232 (1600 hrs)
521 *Thomas Playford* (1445 hrs. Light engine Penfield ex. 670)   Rx218 (2000 hrs)

Tuesday 13/9/1966
Pilots for the day: 523 *Essington Lewis*, Rx193.
Rx228 (0910 hrs. Shunt)
Rx193 (1205 hrs. Bowden ex.368)   Stabling times: Rx228 (1600 hrs)

Thursday 3/11/1966
Pilots for the day: 522 *Sir Malcolm Barclay-Harvey*, Rx228.
Rx225 (0910 hrs. Shunt)   Stabling times: Rx225 (1600 hrs)
Rx158 (1400 hrs. Shunt relieve 0602 hrs shunter)   Rx158 (2000 hrs)

NOTE: When engines were assigned to shunting or pilot duties an allowance of three miles for every hour assigned was calculated as being that engine's daily mileage. So ten hours' pilot service would be recorded as 30 miles 'worked'.

The use of 520 as pilot at Mile End in November 1966 was preceded by its B.I.T. in late September at Islington. Beginning October 11 it ran a series of 'running-in' turns which included a trip to Willunga on the 16.30 hrs goods, and to Penfield on October 12-14, to haul the 16.19 hrs Adelaide passenger service. As a result of 520 coming out of Islington in October, 526 entered the works for a light service and B.I.T. This was to be the last service carried out on a broad gauge engine for retention in *normal* traffic.

One other large power engine in service late in the year was 524 *Sir Mellis Napier* which was the last steam locomotive to work a Port Pirie train in normal service on October 7. It worked to Pirie on the 0800 hrs from Adelaide and returned on the 1725 hrs the same day.

Although the majority of Rx engines were by now infrequently used, apart from pilot duties an Rx occasionally saw service on the 12.05 hrs Mile End-Bowden scrap train. Transfers between Dry Creek or Islington would also see the rare reappearance of steam power, and on October 4 an Rx was used on the Woodville goods, usually a diesel task.

In November Rx5, which had been withdrawn, was moved from Mile End to Kapunda between the 28th and the 30th, to be displayed as a historical exhibit. In December, 621 went to Islington for a 'B' service and passed its B.I.T. in order to work specials in 1967, and despite the general non-use of much steam power, the Myer Santa Specials still saw 521 *Thomas Playford* at the head. It was also, as a result, the first time this class had been used on the Outer Harbor line, fares being 30c adults, 15c for children.

Services and B.I.T.'s

The following engines received services and B.I.T.'s during 1966, so enabling them to remain in traffic for at least one year from date of testing.

February	: Rx224, 718	August	: 521
March	: F255	September	: 520
April	: 700	November	: 526
June	: 522	December	: F170, 621

Due to the fairly low mileages by 1966 some engines were having (with authority from the Boiler Inspector) their B.I.T.'s extended. This was usually calculated on the basis of one month's extension for each inactive month. Consequently engines such as 624 and 752, with boiler certificates issued as far back as 1962 and 1963, were still 'available' for limited use should the need arise.

The last of the '750' class to see regular service, No. 752 lies on the storage rank at Mile End roundhouse in October 1966.
Photo: M. Billett

Engines were usually stabled at Mile End roundhouse with their tenders facing the central turntable. Here four Rx locos (from left, 227, 199, 230 and 224) pose for the camera in October 1966.   Photo: M. Billett

Engines condemned during 1966:

| August | Rx146 | October | Rx93, Rx210, 701, 708, 709 |
| September | Rx197 | | |

1967

An assessment was made of the locomotives at Mile End depot as at 31 January, and the following engines were recorded.

Rx class 4-6-0
9 (condemned, 15, 48 (parked), 56 (parked), 140 (parked), 158 (parked), 160 (overdue B.I.T.), 190 (parked), 192, 193 (overdue B.I.T.), 194 (condemned), 195 (parked), 198 (parked), 199, 200, 202 (overdue B.I.T.), 207 (parked), 208, 209 (parked), 210, 211 (overdue B.I.T.), 212 (overdue B.I.T.), 215 (parked), 217 (parked), 218 (overdue B.I.T.), 222 (parked), 224 (parked), 225, 227 (parked), 228 (overdue B.I.T.), 229 (overdue B.I.T.), 230 (parked), 231 (parked), 232 (parked), 233 (parked).

Total: 35

2nd F class 4-6-2T
170 (at Islington), 171, 180 (Islington), 236, 240 (parked), 244 (parked), 253 (parked), 255.

Total: 8

520 class 4-8-4
520 *Sir Malcolm Barclay-Harvey*
521 *Thomas Playford*
522 *Malcolm McIntosh*
523 *Essington Lewis*
524 *Sir Mellis Napier*
526 *Duchess of Gloucester*

Total: 6

620 class 4-6-2
621, 622 (parked), 624, 625 (overdue B.I.T.), 626 (parked), 627, 628 (parked), 629 (parked)

Total: 8

700/710 class 2-8-2
700, 706, 708 (condemned), 709 (condemned), 717, 718.

Total: 6

750 class
752, 755

Total: 2

ENGINE STATUS

In April 1967 a statement of locomotives at Mile End was made to the Loco Superintendent at Adelaide, and the list showed the condition of engines, and mileages accumulated, since the engine's previous service. The list was current on April 10th, 1967.

No.	Position	B.I.T. due or done	G.O. due	Mileage service last 'D' service	Last service & mileage since
Rx9	condemned	—	1967		
Rx15	in traffic	11/ 3/67	1969	9510	A 4500
Rx48	parked	12/10/67	1967	1320	D
Rx56	parked	1/12/67	1968	22375	C 1190
Rx140	parked	5/10/67	1969	2950	D
Rx158	parked	10/ 6/67	1969	31025	B 2670
Rx160	parked	overdue	1969	40110	B 6110
Rx190	parked	2/ 8/67	1969	6684	B 1300
Rx192	in traffic	22/ 4/67	1967	23445	B 1710
Rx193	parked	overdue	1966	32030	B 4375
Rx194	condemned				
Rx195	parked	19/10/67	1968	19760	C 1960
Rx198	parked	3/ 9/67	1969	12385	B 2040
Rx199	parked	31/ 8/67	1967	17630	C 460
Rx200	parked	overdue	1967	1168	D
Rx202	parked	overdue	1967	35879	B 2359
Rx207	parked	7/11/67	1971	1010	D
Rx208	in traffic	11/ 4/67	1968	2814	D
Rx209	parked	11/ 3/67	1970	34472	C 3022
Rx210	in traffic	14/ 4/67	1967	9684	B 70
Rx211	parked	overdue	1969	35980	A 1810
Rx212	parked	overdue	1968	33957	A 1125
Rx215	parked	19/11/67	1968	28875	B 270
Rx217	parked	1/ 9/67	1969	Nil	D
Rx218	parked	overdue	1968	5170	A 590
Rx222	parked	13/11/67	1968	9227	B 102
Rx224	parked	24/11/67	1970	180	D
Rx225	in traffic	4/ 4/67	1968	21860	C 2974
Rx227	parked	18/10/67	1969		
Rx228	parked	overdue	1968	33108	B 4723
Rx229	parked	overdue	1967	3570	D
Rx230	parked	31/10/67	1968	1455	D
Rx231	parked	1/12/67	1968	25330	C 540
Rx233	condemned				
F170	at works		1967		
F171	in traffic	25/ 9/67	1968	26030	B 1280
F180	at works		1968		
F236	in traffic	11/ 9/67	1967	21065	B 1100
F240	parked	15/10/67	1967	26355	B 125
F244	parked	9/11/67	1968	9220	B 490
F253	parked	27/10/67	1968	22615	B 670
F255	in traffic	11/ 8/67	1968	9220	B 710
520	parked	15/ 9/67	1970	32665	B 825
521	parked	20/ 8/67	1969	1490	D

522	parked	30/ 8/67	1969	290	D	
523	at works	—	1968	32690	C	6785
524	parked	24/ 3/67	1968	40640	C	5245
526	parked	14/11/67	1969	48630	B	150
621	parked	14/12/67	1969	22885	B	Nil
622	parked	31/ 8/66	1968			
624	parked	29/ 3/67	1967	27571	C	4381
625	parked	overdue	1968	12830	B	6445
626	parked	19/ 6/66	1968	19680	A	6620
627	parked	25/ 9/67	1969	27560	B	8195
628	parked	2/ 8/66	1969	31013	B	2385
629	parked	12/12/66	1969	6625	D	
700	parked	28/ 8/67	1967	150	D	
706	parked	9/11/67	1967	39505	B	1505
717	parked	1/11/67	1967	11095	B	2325
718	parked	28/ 8/67	1967	31565	B	2735
752	parked	8/10/67	1969	38640	B	165
755	parked	8/ 5/64	1969	10967	A	3235

G.O.: General Overhaul

Condemned:
The following locomotives were later condemned in September 1967:
Rx15, Rx48, Rx56, Rx192, Rx193, Rx195, Rx199, Rx200, Rx201, Rx202, Rx208, Rx215, Rx222, Rx229, Rx230, Rx231, F180, F236, F240, F244, F253, F255, 625, 626, 627, 628, 629, 700*, 706, 717, 718*, 752, 755.
* Although condemned in 1967, both these engines hauled specials in 1968.

In March 1967 two Rx class engines were still in use as shunters at Terowie (200 and 225), and indeed Rx225 clocked up the highest individual mileage for an engine of its class in both February and March.

On March 26 Rx199 was used on a mystery tour to Clare on behalf of local radio station 5AD. Contestants had to guess the trip destination in order to win a seat on the special train. Pilot engine for the outing was Rx192, and both engines were specially cleaned for the occasion.

With the official closure of Mile End roundhouse from June 30 control of the depot fell under the foreman of the nearby Diesel Depot. On July 3 an Rx engine was noted in steam at the Diesel Depot, and on July 27 F171 and diesel No.506 were engaged in repositioning steam engines at the roundhouse.

By now, apart from Rx shunt engines engaged at Tailem Bend, only F class shunters at Islington works provided any broad gauge steam workings. From August 18, diesel No.350 was allocated to Islington, thus reducing the amount of work for the resident steam shunters. F170 was recorded as being the last steam shunter to be used at the works in November 1967, and as if to finalise the change-over, diesel No.351 was sent to Islington on January 23, 1968 as supplementary shunter.

Final monthly mileages of engines, 1967.

Engine No.	Jan	Feb	March	April	May	June	July	August	Sept	Oct	Nov	Dec	TOTAL
F class	83*	209*	178*	129*	360	330	338*	311*	137*	254	96	—	4899
Rx class	152*	145*	149*	74*	101*	96*	48*	66	68*	69	58	14	4990
523	—	—	—	—	—	—	28	—	—	—	—	—	28
526	—	—	—	—	—	—	—	32	257	—	—	—	289
621	—	—	—	—	139	68	167	—	170	—	—	—	544
700	—	—	—	—	—	28	—	102	—	—	—	—	130
718	—	—	—	—	—	182	—	—	50	24	—	—	74

'F' class 4-6-2T No.170 was the last Islington shunter recorded as being used in November 1967, and so became the last steam engine to be used in regular traffic in the Adelaide area. It is seen here at Islington on March 17, 1967.   Photo: S.A. McNicol

NOTES: *Denotes *average* mileages for the class, with various members of stud contributing small mileages toward total.

F class engines working over the year included: 180, 244 in January, 170, 171 and 180 February, 170, 171, 180 and 255 March, 170, 171, 180, 253 and 255 April, 253 May and June, 170 and 253 July, 170 and 253 August, 170, 171 and 253 September, 171 October, and 170 finally in November.

Eight Rx engines worked in January with Rx225 clocking up the highest mileage (440 miles), nine worked in February (Rx225 top with 373 miles), eight in March (Rx225 top with 261 miles), six in April (Rx199 top, 121 miles) while May to July only two engines worked each month (Rx214, 102 miles May; Rx235, 118 miles July). By then only Tailem Bend had working Rx engines employed, using Rx214 and 235 in July and September, but Rx214 alone in August, November and December, while Rx235 was used solely in October. The use of Rx214 on December 1, 1967, was the last occasion a broad gauge steam locomotive was employed by S.A.R. for ordinary revenue service.

Of the remaining locomotives used, 621 worked two arranged freights to Willunga early in the year and one *special* passenger job up to June, with the remaining mileages being accumulated on Penfield test runs and special passenger trains. Remaining engines all accumulated their mileages on, or as a consequence of, impending special train workings.

Islington works

The following engines were noted at the workshops during 1967. Many of the engines had come to be cut up. Some, however, such as Nos. 700/718, 523 and 526 were visitors in order to remain trafficable.

February 14	708	October 31	Rx216, F170, F171, F253
March 2	709	November 4	700, 718
March 15	F170, F180, 523 *Essington Lewis*		

Removal of locomotives from the roundhouse

Following the end of revenue earning steam operation on the South Australian broad gauge in 1967, a number of steam operated railtours were organised by the Australian Railway Historical Society. The final two extant Mikados (Nos. 700 and 718) ran a number of railtours to commemorate their impending demise, culminating in a final double-headed run from Victor Harbor to Mount Barker Junction on June 2, 1968. By August 25, 1968 Rx207 and Rx224 were at Mile End Diesel Depot signalling their association with the ARHS as railtour engines, while fellow class members rusted or accumulated dust inside and outside the rapidly crumbling old roundhouse.

Among noted engines at the roundhouse earlier in the previous month were the following locomotives: Rx227, Rx194, Rx48, Rx160, Rx229, 622, 626 and 629.

In October 1968 both 523 *Essington Lewis* and 526 *Duchess of Gloucester* were at Mile End Diesel Depot in preparation for railtours, the former engine would soon finish such duties as it was the class representative earmarked for the Mile End Railway Museum. Both engines had been observed earlier in the year, being prepared for duties, at Islington works.

On June 5 three Rx engines (200, 202 and 228) were hauled to Islington for cutting up from the roundhouse, while on June 26 diesel No.845 hauled Pacifics No.625 and 628 on their final trip to Islington. Rx216 with six-wheel tender was sent from Islington (where it had been stored for many years) back to Mile End. Mikados Nos. 700 and 718 were towed to Islington for cutting on 9/8/68. The boiler house at Mile End was demolished in 1968, while over towards Railway Terrace the site of the demolished straight-through depot was having the S.A. Cold Stores building erected. Rx198 was sent to supply steam at Diesel Depot on January 15, when the depot's ordinary boiler was out of use. It was there again on March 11.

The following engines were still at the roundhouse at the end of 1968: 622 and 629 (outside the north end), Rx207, 526 *Duchess of Gloucester*, Rx231, Rx215, Rx190, Rx218, Rx232, 627, Rx56, Rx210, Rx209, Rx140, 520 *Sir Malcolm Barclay-Harvey*, 521 *Thomas Playford*, 522 *Malcolm McIntosh*, Rx224, 524 *Sir Mellis Napier*, Rx195, Rx158, Rx217, Rx216, Rx208, Rx215, Rx227, Rx194, Rx48, Rx160, Rx229, Rx198, Rx212, Rx225, Rx211. Pacific No.626 which had also been at the depot was hauled to Islington for cutting on December 23.

On a happier note, F245, which had been withdrawn as long ago as November 1959, and had been stored at the eastern side of Gawler station, was finally put on display near the Gawler Bowling Club. With the aid of the wrecking crane Rotary Club members shifted it to its present Victoria Terrace site. The locomotive had clocked up an impressive 1,038,203 miles when retired in 1959.

Rx212 in open storage at Mile End on June 22, 1968. This engine was overdue on its B.I.T. the previous year and was condemned on August 20, 1968.
Photo: S.A. McNicol

During 1968 and 1969 locomotives continued to be scrapped at Islington, but because of the large number of broad gauge engines retained in storage during the mid 'sixties, it was a long process. In June 1969, no less than 27 engines were still recorded stored or condemned at Mile End roundhouse. Engines noted were:

Rx class
56, 140, 158, 160, 190, 194, 195, 198, 208, 209, 210, 211, 212, 215, 216, 217, 218, 225, 227, 229, 231, 232, 233.

520 class
520 *Sir Malcolm Barclay-Harvey*　　　522 *Malcolm McIntosh*
521 *Thomas Playford*　　　　　　　　524 *Sir Mellis Napier*

At Tailem Bend four other Rx 4-6-0s were still in storage besides the Rx No.201, which had been offered a permanent residency in the town as a preservation piece. The stored Rx engines were: Nos. 214, 219, 155 and 235.

These four were soon to be called for scrapping, however, as the S.A.R. Institute magazine recorded that the last Rx engines were removed from Tailem Bend depot on July 27, 1969, when they were hauled to Islington by diesel No.957. (The magazine mistakenly recorded the engines as Nos. 155, 215, 219 and 235).

Besides the locomotives stored at the two above depots, four other engines still remained from the broad gauge fleet. Rx207 and Rx224 were by now being used on railtours for the ARHS together with 526 *Duchess of Gloucester*, while Pacific No.621 was still stored out of service at Islington workshops.

In October 1969 Rx231 was moved to Mile End Diesel Depot in preparation for its move to a park in Kadina as a preservation exhibit. *Duchess of Gloucester* became one of the last broad gauge engines to visit Terowie depot when she ran there on an ARHS special later in the month.

Among the engines awaiting cutting-up at Islington on November 12, 1969 were: Rx215, 232, 198 and 190 with 524 *Sir Mellis Napier*.

Final withdrawals of all non-railtour operating broad gauge steam engines was completed during 1969 with the following condemnations:

February 1969　　　　August 1969
Rx158　　　　　　　　Rx140, 160, 209, 219, 227 and 235.
　　　　　　　　　　　521 *Thomas Playford*, 523 *Essington Lewis*, 524 *Sir Mellis Napier*.

THE LAST OF THE 'BIG POWER'

In early January No.521 arrived at Islington for cutting up, and by the end of the month 520 and 522 had also arrived. However, 520 was spared the torch as it was retained for eventual replacement of No.526 as a railtour engine for the ARHS. Pacific No.621, still stored at Islington, was soon to be the object of a successful restoration project by the ARHS. In May, Rx216 (complete with six-wheel tender and copper capped chimney) and Rx160 were at the works and both were earmarked for preservation. The latter engine eventually went to Murray Bridge, to be exhibited beside the river, while 216 had been earmarked for Elizabeth city display from the early 1960s when it was withdrawn. By 1969 SAR considered displaying the engine at the Railway's Oval, Adelaide, but nothing came of it.

All but three tracks were removed from Mile End loco depot area during Easter 1970, one of the lines running under the soon to be demolished coal stage, with the other two going into the rapidly deteriorating roundhouse. Tenders were called in July 1970 for the demolition and removal of the public coal staiths at Mile End, and the demolition and removal of the concrete coal gantry at Tailem Bend depot.

The final levelling of the roundhouse site was a protracted affair, and as late as March 1974 the locoshed was still recognisable for what it had once been — virtually fifty years after construction on the shed had started. By now the locos had long gone, so too the turntable that led to the radiating stalls. Curiously, in the final demolition phase the depot took on a similar appearance to that it had displayed nearly fifty years previously, with stacks of trackwork inside the arena of skeletal timberwork.

As loose galvanised iron flapped in the wind, and weeds continued to take over what little remained of the visible trackwork, it became harder to imagine that once hundreds of men had been employed at the site, and that some of Australia's largest steam locomotives had once been housed in the now derelict stalls. Mile End roundhouse, like most of its engines, has gone. Happily, a memory remains in the form of preserved engines, fittingly less than ¼ mile from the site, at the Mile End Railway Museum.

Mile End Roundhouse at the very end. These two pictures taken in March 1974 show the stalls, some offices and turntable pit in various stages of demolition.
Photos: S.A. McNicol

THE MEN OF MILE END

No book on the roundhouse at Mile End would be complete without some reference to the men who worked there, either as enginemen or maintenance and administration staff. During the twilight years of the roundhouse leading personalities included Norm Pelton and Horrie Caruthers, Loco Foreman and Shed Foreman respectively, with Bill Shard, Arthur Vivian, Jimmy Dixon and Eric Webster their sub-foremen in descending authority.

The comments following, from staff that used to work at the depot, come from people no longer connected with depot life. Yet although 'retired', so vivid are their recollections of the days of steam, many gave the impression they were working at Mile End roundhouse only the other week. As for example, Arthur Vivian (sub-foreman at Mile End until 1965) said steam had its own charm.

"I never took any interest in diesels at all. I was brought up with steam, 49 years in the job . . . When the diesels came that settled me. I didn't want anything to do with them. There's something with steam that grips you. You're listening all the time in case something's going to go wrong. And you can pick it straight away. Whereas with diesels you've got to be a Philadelphia lawyer to understand them."

Not that engine crews had an easy life. They had to maintain schedules, guard their boiler from running short of water or steam, and also make sure they had enough fuel to make it home, as driver Frank Knowling (retired 1972) recollects.

"We're coming home on a freight train one day with 729, and we're coming down through Islington, going like a scalded cat. My mate says, 'The fire's gone out, boy.' And I said, 'Why?' 'Got no bloody oil.' I said everything will be apple-pie, as long as they don't hold us at the Gaol Loop, and the stick's off. Right round to Mile End Yard we went. But we had to get an engine to pull us into Mile End (roundhouse)."

Luck is sometimes on the side of crews when they get into tight situations, but Frank Knowling must have thought that he was having an exceptionally bad run of luck when the stoker failed one day he was firing a '500' class back from Victor Harbor.

"Coming home one day with 507 . . . and the stoker stopped. I'm shovelling the damned coal into her from Port Elliot right to Mount Barker. A 500 is an awkward engine to fire because you can't get into the back corners. I'd been trying the stoker all the way from Victor in between firing. All sorts we had to do. Going up to Mount Barker Junction I turned on the bloody stoker and away she went, as if nothing had happened!"

The stoker, of course, shouldn't have failed, and special precautions were taken at the coal gantry at Mile End to ensure that any coal for stoker-fired engines was of a suitable size to negotiate the channel between tender and firebox. Neil Head, also a driver at the roundhouse, explains the screening process, for what it was worth.

"When it went into the gantry . . . they had a grate, and the coal that wouldn't go through that grate they'd have to crack with a hammer, and let it go through. And it was quite all right. The stoker would take it."

A very dangerous situation in any railway operation is when a train becomes derailed. Apart from the damage usually caused to engine, track and permanent way, the crew and often passengers are in danger of serious injury. A Mile End driver recalls a lucky escape many years ago.

"603, she turned over one day on the Saddleworth. She was coming from Saddleworth to Manoora when she hit a few sleepers or bolts . . . and turned right over on her side. Nobody got hurt. A bloke was sitting in the second carriage, I think, and he's sitting on the toilet, and a rail went up between him. If he'd been standing up it'd have knocked him off."

Enginemen the world over recall the special relationship that existed with the steam engine and its crew. Preferences and favourites always existed, with some types of engine preferred over others, sometimes for obvious advantages of convenience or comfort, but sometimes for no apparent reason. Drivers on the S.A.R. broad gauge had similar likes and dislikes, and often the idiosyncrasies of one class or another were put up with a shrug of the shoulders. Older drivers remember the 'S' class before the arrival of the Webb 'big engines', when they were in charge of the Melbourne expresses as far as Serviceton. Legend is the reputation of the class for extraordinary turns of speed, often coupled double-headed. Then shaker grates were fitted in their later life, besides alterations to their ash pan and smokebox. Grease was increasingly used in place of oil for lubrication, the result as Arthur Vivian pointed out:

> "They spoilt them. They would not run, they wouldn't coast after that. But when they were on oil they would coast for mile after mile."

The more modern power that superseded the earlier types such as the 'S' class was much appreciated by engine crews, sometimes to such an extent that efforts to 'fail' older engines on rosters were sometimes attempted. Displaced by the Webb big engines on premier turns, classes such as the 'S' were used on lesser duties such as the Gladstone passenger. One staff explained the Gladstone:

> "Used to be run with an 'S' class, and an 'S' class was harder to work than a '620'. And they used to do something to the engine and try to get the pilot engine (which would be a '620'). Ah, there was a lot of tricks in the trade!"

The bigger version of the '620', the '600' class Pacifics, were equally as popular before their displacement by diesels in the late 1950s. Neil Head remembers well his days driving them.

> "Honest as the day is long, but hellish and rough to ride on. They were supposed to be well compensated by big six foot wheels and all that . . . A good engine to handle. You could get 80 mile and hour out of them. Once the firemen knew the engine it was all right, but if he let it get down a bit it was pretty hard work. Around 300 baskets of coal (would be used) between Terowie and Adelaide . . . and from Serviceton to Tailem Bend you'd use 150 baskets of coal. There'd be about 10 shovelfuls in a basket."

The Mikados lasted a little while longer than their large Pacific counterparts, with even a few of the '700' class lasting into the mid-1960s. The present secretary of the A.F.U.L.E., Rex Mathews, himself a fireman at one time at Mile End is quite proud of his asscciation with the class, despite misgivings about some other broad gauge types.

> "I handled those fairly well. Some of the enginemen . . . with whom I worked, were pleasantly surprised that I was able to maintain the steam pressure in the fire of those . . . very easily."

He was equally as praiseworthy of the '500' class engines, which with their stokers, greatly reduced a lot of effort required by the firemen, but introduced a new skill.

> "Physically, there wasn't a great deal of trouble, except when the coal began to run out . . . you might have to pull a little coal forward. Watching of the two elevating screws which faced you inside the cab, and the adjusting of air which sprayed the coal into the firebox was quite an art."

Of the older types of classes around in the final years of broad gauge steam, the 'P' class were the first to disappear. Consequently only the older drivers remember them from the days when they would handle light passenger duties. By the end of 1957 of course, all were condemned. Neil Head remembers them as:

> "Beautiful old engines. When the Glenelg line was still open we used to fill them up with lumps at South Terrace and nearly go to the Bay, and you wouldn't put a fire on. They finished up . . . with one at Mile End and it was shunter . . . for the Dollies, shifting them from one bay to the other. It couldn't pull the big engines though — it would slip too much."

The long serving Rx and F class (the Dollies) were well liked by crews, and of the people I've spoken to, few have expressed any real criticism, a view no doubt reflected in the fact that examples of both classes survived right up to the end of broad gauge steam use. Not so, however, the '750' class Mikados which were imported from Victorian Railways in the early 1950s. Most drivers disliked them, if only for their antiquated cab controls, which must have seemed primitive in comparison to S.A.R. Mikados. One driver described them perhaps fairly.

Engine servicing facilities at branchline terminals offered the barest essentials to enable engines to safely complete their return trip. Peebinga was no exception. On one of its last trips Rx201, coming off the triangle at 7 am, was almost hidden from view by the low Mallee scrub surrounding the station on October 12, 1965. Photo: J.G. Southwell

Although officially condemned in April 1960, '720' class No.735 was withdrawn from service some years previously and sat forlornly on a short spur opposite Mile End coal gantry until scrapped. Photo: J.G. Southwell

> "They were an honest old engine . . . they weren't hard to fire or anything, but they were a lousy engine to ride on and look out of the side. And then you had to get off your seat all the time to be able to do anything . . ."

The class was doomed to a short life of course. With the introduction of S.A.R.'s first mainline diesels occurring concurrently with their purchase from Victoria, the die was already cast for dieselisation. But a steam engine still had some benefits that the new motive power lacked.

> "We used to go to Gladstone . . . used to put our bikes on the back of the tender, and when we got to Gladstone, had a shower and a cup of tea we'd push the bikes to Laura. Stop at my Aunty's place . . . have a cup of tea with her, and then we'd push them on to Stone Hut."

This 'taking your wheels with you' also proved handy if you were a crew sent to country centres, such as Wallaroo for a fortnight.

The rapid acceleration in dieselising the S.A.R. broad gauge in the 60s meant that old skills were disappearing as quickly as new ones were being introduced, as one shed staff member put it:

> "As far as I was concerned there was nothing different much. But once the diesels came, the steam went out and that was the biggest . . . change as far as I was concerned. But I'd sooner work on steam than diesel."

Some ex-drivers such as Neil Head spent their later years training young drivers how to handle diesels. The contrasts must have been quite large, to the work of firemen in earlier days.

> "I've put 150 baskets (of coal) on at Riverton with a shovel. Shovel it into a basket, and then put the basket up in the gangway and then carry it and tip it in. The lads today sitting on the diesels, and sitting there reading the blasted book while he's going along. I used to say to them, 'Bloody kids don't know what work is!' But then again it's all gone advanced. I mean you can't go backwards. And thirty, forty or fifty years time, they'll be back to steam — don't worry about that."

Finally it might be asked what enabled some railway employees to recollect events and incidents of fifteen, twenty and even fifty years ago, with such amazing clarity. Their jobs as enginemen, fitters, signalmen or even guards couldn't have been easy, and the salary hardly princely. Perhaps it was the responsibility that their jobs entailed, the safety and dependability assumed by their service, and perhaps it came from the comradeship that developed while on the job.

> "Some of the blokes that you work with, you work with them all of your life. Like we're in the railways for 49 years each. Well, we're working together all the time . . . You see them every day of your life, you'd see them more than you did your own wife."

GLOSSARY OF TERMS

In various parts of this book reference is made to many points of an engine's anatomy. For the uninitiated the following 'abridged dictionary of locomotive bits-and-pieces' is offered.

Ashpan
These are fitted under the firebox, and they collect ash that falls through the grate. Some ashpans are shaped in the form of a hopper, with either sliding or hinged bottom doors from which to empty ash. Doors must always be closed while the loco is in operation. The pan is fitted with a wetter, operated from the cab to prevent dust ash about the engine, and the depositing of hot ashes in the pit or track. There have been instances in the past when technically sound loco designs have fallen short of expected potential, due to inadequate air circulation within the ashpan and grate area.

Berkshire
Locomotives with the 2-8-4 wheel formation, and in South Australia the '720' class. An American term said to have derived from the first locos to enter service over the Berkshire Hills, on the Boston and Albany Railway.

Blowdown valves
Are valves fitted to the outside shell of the firebox at the lowest possible point of the foundation ring. They are operated from rodding controlled from the cab, and are used to reduce the silt deposits and salt concentrations before and after a journey, and also in accordance with loco instructions. On S.A.R. locos used in shunting yards the side blowdown was modified so that water was directed to track centre, and the steam upwards.

Blower valve
Is operated from the cab by a wheel with the valve in the smokebox. It directs a jet of live steam up the chimney, as near central as possible, thus producing a partial vacuum in the smokebox, which in turn creates a draught through the tubes, firebox and grate. Used while the engine is standing, it stops gases from entering the cab.

Booster
A small additional cylinder or cylinders mounted above the trailing wheels beneath the firebox, and used to 'boost' the total available power of the loco. Usually only employed at starting or for short bursts of extremely arduous working, it was fitted to the '500' class and some Mikados (though later removed) and in the former it improved tractive effort by some 8,000 lbs.

Brick arch
Is composed of several rows of special fire bricks laid in arch form. Its position prevents the fuel gases escaping too quickly from the firebox, so bringing about more complete combustion. It protects the tubeplate from cold draughts of air when the firedoor is open, besides helping to maintain an even temperature in the firebox and acts as a spark arrester. The collapse of the arch would effect the steaming abilities of an engine greatly.

Clothing
The thermal wrapping that surrounds a boiler to retain the heat. In the past this has usually been of an asbestos-type wrap, then being covered by an outer shell of light metal sheeting. Recent thermal wraps on preserved steam engines have been of a glass-fibre type, similar to those employed in home insulation.

Connecting rod
The rod that links the coupling rod on the wheels, with the crosshead on the slidebars, and thus the piston from the cylinders.

Coupling rod
The rod that connects the wheels and makes them turn through means of the crank.

Crown stays
Are used to support the firebox crown sheet plate to the outside shell of the firebox making the water space and preventing these sheets from buckling through heat. (See also stays).

Cut-off
Is that part of the stroke at which the slide valve closes the steam port. It is obtained by means of a lap on the slide valve. Cutting off steam earlier in the stroke of the piston, it permits live steam admitted into the cylinders to expand down to a lower pressure before exhausting. This obtains more work out of it.

Cylinder and steam chest drain valves
Are fitted to the lowest part of the cylinder to allow water formed by condensed steam to drain out of the cylinders. All locos are fitted with two such valves, one at each end of the cylinders.

Dampers
Are hinged plates fitted below the level of the grate. Operated from the cab, they are used to regulate the flow of air to the fire and so control steam pressure while the regulator is closed.

Dome
This is a receptacle for steam situated on the highest point of the boiler as a collecting area for dry

steam. Usually central on the boiler barrel, where the regulator valve is usually sited, some locomotives didn't employ a dome (the argument being it weakened overall boiler strength) and in these cases a perforated pipe running just inside the top of the boiler was substituted.

Fusible plugs
These are a safety device to protect the boiler against water shortage. A brass plug is drilled lengthwise and then the hole is filled with lead or a bullet is inserted, supported by a lead thimble. This plug is screwed into the crown sheet of the firebox. While the plug and crown sheet is covered with water the lead is kept below melting point, and if it becomes uncovered the heat of the firebox melts the lead thus allowing steam into the firebox, assisting in the extinguishing of the fire and drawing the attention of the crew.

Hot box
The overheating of an axlebox on a loco. In general the axlebox is a block of metal with a semi-circular recess lined with bronze on its underside. The bronze (or brass) is partially lined with 'white metal' which softens and eases situations where local overloading of the sliding surfaces of the bronze and the axle can occur. The surfaces are supplied with small quantities of oil, preferably from underneath rather than on top of the box, to prevent overheating, usually noticed by a burning-oil smell.

Injectors
Are used to supply water to the loco from its tender through a series of co-axial cones, which permit steam to leave the boiler and suck up cold water, take it warmed back into the boiler. Once 'set' the injector has no moving parts and therefore uses no power. Injectors can be put out of action by solids in the water supply, failure of both (usually only one is used at a time) can necessitate drastic action in dropping a fire in order to avoid boiler damage. Reasons for faulty injectors can include dirt or scale on injector cones, or excessive wear or distortion there. Air leaks in water supply, air drawn in with the feed water causing bubbles which break up the jet, can also make injectors fail. If the feed water is too hot, the delivery pipe becomes choked with scale or the clack valve is not seating properly, or if a defect in the connection to the coal watering pipe occurs further injector problems become apparent.

Mechanical lubricator
Is usually mounted on the footplate and is operated to lubricate the valves and pistons, and any other moving parts through a ratchet and pawl from a moving part of the valve gear.

Mountain
Locos of a 4-8-2 wheel formation, said to be derived from a series of engines built by the U.S. Chesapeake and Ohio Railway. In South Australia the '500' class originally started out as 4-8-2 types until an extra axle was added to the rear, carrying the booster. Although they became by definition "Northerns", the '500' class retained the "Mountain" tag.

Oils
There are generally two types of oil used: engine oil as used on bearings etc., or where trimmings are used; and cylinder oil which is used on valves, pistons, compressors and so on. This type of oil is too heavy to pass through trimmings unless the bearings are very hot. It is used in sight feed lubricators as engine oil flash point is too low, and if used in lubricators it would carbonise in steam chests and cylinders.

Outside and inside admission
Outside admission valves are those in which the steam has to pass the outside edge of the valve to enter the steam port. Inside admission valves are those in which the steam has to pass the inside edge to enter the steam port. Piston valves may be either inside or outside admission.

Pacific
Another terminology defining wheel formation, in this case 4-6-2 notation. In South Australia this included the '600', '620' and 2nd 'F' class tanks.

Pean (also pane, peen or pein)
The opposite end of a hammerhead to that carrying the face, made to various shapes for particular types of work (e.g. rivetting etc.).

Priming
Boiler priming is one of the most objectionable features in loco working and results in extensive damage by fracturing cylinder covers and loosening piston heads, besides washing lubrication from valve chambers and cylinder walls, causing additional coal consumption and engine inefficiency. It is sometimes caused by carrying too much water. If however water level is low it may be caused by the solids which are in the boiler and foaming thus causing a scum on top of the water, in turn being carried into the cylinders and valves.

Regulator valve
The valve placed in the dome or steam space of an engine which is operated by a handle in the cab, and serves to control steam supply to the cylinders.

Rocking grates
Consist of a number of hinged grates having holes or slots through the plates to allow the air to pass through by means of rods. Connected to the underside of the plates they may be rocked or partially rotated. This is achieved by a handle in the cab; when shaken the ashes fall into the ashpan. The section of the grate near the tube-plate is made to tilt downwards so large pieces of clinker can be pushed by fireirons into the ashpan.

Route availability
Limit, or not, of the lines that a certain type of locomotive could work over safely. In South Australia this was determined by the Chief Engineer who took into consideration factors of axle weight of the engine, weight of track (say 60 lb or 80 lb) and clearances and expected speeds, besides ability of bridges to carry the engine weight.

Safety valves
Are to safeguard the boiler against overpressure of steam. Two or more are always provided, as one may not be equal to the task. They should never be interfered with by unqualified persons. On a loco with two safety valves, i.e. one blows off at 175 lbs sq. in., the other at 180 lbs sq. in.

Sight feed lubricator
Is an oil vessel, to the top of which is attached a condensing globe from which, to a point near the bottom of the vessel is fixed an internal pipe, also an internal pipe from each sight feed glass to a point near the top of the oil vessel and valves, viz steam, water retention and regulating valves. It is used to lubricate the valves and pistons with cylinder oil.

Smokebox
The large chamber which rests, and is rigidly secured to the engine framing, and supports the front end of the barrel. It has an opening at the top for the chimney. It also contains the main steam pipes, the exhaust or blast pipe, blower and spark arrestors or screens. The door must be correctly fitted and closed tightly to prevent air entering the smokebox and affecting the steaming qualities.

Spark arrestors
Are in the form of meshwire that ensures that only the very small pieces of cinders escape from the smokebox, giving less likelihood of starting fires. Arresters must be examined when starting and finishing a journey to ensure that no holes exist, or openings in the plates.

Stays
The firebox of a loco includes many flat, or almost flat surfaces, which under the effect of high steam pressure would buckle and collapse if unsupported. The flat top of a firebox and the almost flat sides are therefore stayed to the outside shell. Girder stays run longitudinally the length of the firebox crown plate, and are fixed to it, and are slung by means of sling stays to the outer wrapper. Flexible stays are

used in the hottest part of the firebox where there is a differential expansion of the plates of the inner and outer firebox. Flexibility is achieved by the inclusion of a ball and socket joint at one end.

Steam chest
The housing for the valves, usually cast and sometimes integral with the cylinder casting itself. The proportions of the steam chest are of some importance to thermodynamic performance of the loco.

Stoker
A mechanical method of firing large locos, as opposed to hand-firing. Usually achieved by a screw mechanism that extracts the coal from the tender through a pipe into the firegrate. Stokers were fitted to larger South Australian locos, greatly reducing the workload on the fireman.

Superheater elements
The temperature at which water is evaporated (makes steam) depends on the pressure — but at any pressure the steam is always 'wet' or saturated. By superheating this wet steam is dried, resulting in some 25 per cent economy in coal consumption. A 'header' in the smokebox takes steam from the regulator and distributes it through a series of firetubes larger than usual boiler flues. Inside these tubes are the elements in which steam from the header flows back to the firebox, and then by return bend back to header and chest. Steam at say 225 lb sq. in. (at 397°F) enters the header and in passing through the elements, returns to the header at about 600°F, having been superheated by just over 200°F, or an increase in volume of almost 35 per cent.

Syphons
Used to increase the firebox heating surface and increase the speed of circulation of water in the boiler. Improves boiler efficiency by up to 10 per cent, but like superheater elements, syphons present yet another maintenance charge.

Tractive effort (or power)
The mathematical formula for working out power available, usually expressed in thousands of pounds (weight). Taking in factors of boiler pressure, cylinder number and size, driving wheel diameter and so on, it is usually at maximum when an engine is starting from rest.

Trimmings
Plug types are made from looping worsted lengthwise along a piece of twisted copper wire to the desired thickness, and are used on bearings having sufficient rotary or oscillating movement. Tail trimmings are made by threading strands of worsted through a small loop at the end of a piece of twisted copper wire. This type of trimming supplies oil by capillary action, and is used on bearings having little movement to throw oil over the syphon pipe.

Tubeplate
There is one in the firebox and another at the smokebox end of the boiler barrel between which the tubes are supported. The tubeplates are rivetted to the boiler shell, or on later boilers it is permissible to have them welded in.

Valve gears
The Allan and Stephenson valve gears are always placed inside the engine frame, and the Walshaert and Baker Pilliod valve gears are placed outside.

Washout plugs
Plugs that are removed at washout periods to permit flushing of water passages, which are then screwed back into place.

Water gauges
Glass tubes fitted between two brass mountings attached to the face plate of the firebox. Their purpose is to show water level in the boiler. The top mounting contains the steam cock and is connected to the water space. Under the glass is a blow through or try cock used to test the gauges for the water level, or to clean the same. The water level to be carried on level track should be about half-glass,

down grades one-third, up grades three-quarters or sometimes a full glass. Water should never be out of sight in the bottom of the glass as this exposes the crown sheet and fusible plugs.

CLASS HISTORIES

2nd F class
These Pacific tanks are differentiated from the 1st F tanks which were 4-4-0s, condemned some ten years before the introduction of the 2nd F in 1902. Known as "Dollys" the tanks worked all suburban lines on passenger duties, working as far north on occasions as Hamley Bridge in the early days and as far south as Willunga. With the introduction of suburban railcars in the 1950s and 60s fewer of the engines were required, and among their last duties was shunting at Islington workshops. The possibility of a 2nd F tank back in traffic cannot be completely ruled out following the transfer of one of the preserved examples from Elizabeth West to the "Steamranger" tour depot at Dry Creek.

P class
Twenty handsome tank engines built by Beyer-Peacock (6) and James Martin of Gawler (14) between 1884 and 1893, and decidedly as British in design as later Webb engines were identifiable as American. They were built to cope with increased traffic on the Adelaide-Port Adelaide line, and in fact had an association with the Port area to the end of their active lives. They also saw passenger duty on the Semaphore and Glenelg lines until loads became too heavy in later years. First *final* condemnations were begun as early as 1929 though survivors of the class saw much specialised dock area work until the mid-1950s when the introduction of the '800' class diesels displaced them. One engine each was assigned as depot shunter to Mile End and Tailem Bend in the 1950s. The closure of Port Adelaide depot in 1957 also saw the end of the P class with final withdrawal taking place in December 1957. Luckily one example was saved for posterity at Mile End Railway Museum.

Rx class
A development of the earlier 'R' class ten wheelers of 1886, 30 of the class actually being rebuilt from the early design, with a further 54 new engines being added from 1909. The locomotives worked virtually every line on the South Australian broad gauge system, at one time even the Adelaide-Melbourne expresses as far as Murray Bridge. Following the introduction of the Webb superpower they enjoyed many years on secondary duties and light branch working. Yet even into the early 1960s were useful on high mileage duties. The class was employed right up to the end of steam working in 1967, often shunting Mile End yards. Besides the two 'on the books' Rx, a number have been preserved throughout the state, many at locations they were long associated with.

S class
Three members of this class of 18 remained on the books in 1960, not being officially condemned until April. Until the introduction of the large power in the mid-1920s the 'S' class were the principal express type in South Australia. They were often used on expresses to the border beyond Tailem Bend, and also worked as far north as Terowie. In later life they confined their services to the Moonta or Barmera lines, and their last duties were in the South-East of the state. Despite their popularity with enthusiasts no example was saved the cutter's torch.

500 class
The ultimate in broad gauge passenger power was the '500' class 4-8-4s. When introduced in 1926 they revolutionised heavy Hills train haulage with their massive tractive effort, despite some early teething problems always associated with new types. They saw service on the "Overland" service as far as Tailem Bend, besides working as far north as Terowie and Port Pirie, and south to Victor Harbor. When finally ousted from the Hills line in the late 1950s, they didn't have the route availability of the later '520' type, and among their final passenger duties were railfan excursions.

Ex-Victorian Railways 'N' No. 465, as SAR No. 753 takes water at Mile End in the mid-1950s. The '750' class ranged far and wide and were often found on yard transfer runs between Mile End, Port Adelaide and Dry Creek.
Photo: J. G. Southwell

SAR '520' 4-8-4 No. 529 was withdrawn in 1960 following the need to attend to crown stays. In this 1950 view the sleek speedster has her fuel tank topped up with "Bunker C" fuel oil before backing up for further attention from her crew.
Photo: J. G. Southwell

520 class
Loosely based on an American design (Pennsylvania T1) these 'light' 4-8-4s were intended to work lines that were too light to carry the heavier 500s. Designed for both passenger and goods haulage these sleek engines performed their duties admirably. Later members of the class (from 523 onwards) had a slightly modified buffer front, from the more rounded earlier class members. Used to Moonta and Angaston and lines to Terowie and Port Pirie, they also ran to Mount Gambier once the broad gauge was extended there. Their light axle loading enabled them to run on 60 lb rail, and they worked the Pinnaroo and Barmera lines. One of their last regular rosters was the Port Pirie express which they intermittently headed until the mid-1960s.

600 class
Three members of this class of ten engines remained in January 1960. They were part of the Webb modernisation of broad gauge power during the 1920s, and were used on both the "Overland" express, and fast goods trains between Tailem Bend and Serviceton. Because of their relatively high axle loading the 600 class Pacifics were confined to the Victor Harbor, Terowie and Port Pirie lines apart from the mainline to the border. Like the 500 class, the 600s were hampered by this restricted route availability, and all had been withdrawn by the end of 1961. None have been preserved.

620 class
This class of Pacific was to the 600s what the 520s were to the 500 class. With their lighter axle loading the 620s could traverse most South Australian broad gauge areas, and had a good turn of speed besides. From the 1940s the class became established as regular residents of Tailem Bend depot and worked the Murray Lands trains and services to the south-east. Some locomotives were retained at Mile End depot however, and the class usually worked on all lines except the Spalding, Truro and Milang routes. No.621 was named "Duke of Edinburgh" on its return to traffic in 1971, following an appeal by the Australian Railway Historical Society. It had previously languished at Islington workshops for a number of years. It is presently out of service.

700 class / 710 class
These almost identical classes were a design of Mikados intended to work goods trains over 60 lb track, where the larger and heavier Mountain and Pacifics could not venture. They were as a result mainly used on lines such as the Moonta, Gladstone, Morgan, Victor Harbor, Renmark and Pinnaroo. Despite being intended for goods work, both classes enjoyed a regular sortie out on passenger, usually the Hills line. Due to their relatively light axle loadings both types of Mikado still saw work well into the mid-1960s, being employed on trains to Willunga, Robertstown and even Tailem Bend. No.700 and 718 were used on ARHS special trains during 1968, and then were cut-up.

720 class
Six members of this class of 17 freight locomotives remained at the start of 1960, though it was to be their last year on the books. The freight equivalent of the 500 class 4-8-4s, the 720 class were intended as alternatives to extra 710 class Mikados with the extra pair of wheels in these "Berkshires" intended to make the locos available for service on the lighter lines. In practice, however, it was found the class was still too heavy for these lines, and the class was eventually banned from all but the heavier routes. A further restriction placed on the class was their inability to be turned on 75 foot turntables, such as existed at Renmark. The class was built in two batches, 720-4 between 1930-1, and 725-36 between 1938-43. The early 1950s were this class's Indian Summer and by the late 50s most were ready for scrapping, though a few did last 'on the books' until April 1960.

740 class
These Mikados were ordered by the Commonwealth for Railway Rehabilitation in China, and were constructed by Clyde Engineering NSW. With the Communist takeover in China, however, the engines never left the country and the Australian government was left with 50 locos to dispose of. Ten engines became the 'L' class on the Commonwealth, and South Australian Railways, desperately short of motive power, bought a further ten making them the 740 class. Entering service from 1952 they were the last

Rx217 was a Tailem Bend engine for many years until sent up to Islington for a service on August 31, 1965. Following the service the engine is pictured shunting at Charlick's sidings Mile End on October 20, 1965. This loco is one of ten surviving Rx class — this example being sited at Nuriootpa.
Photo: J. Wilson

The straight shed at Mile End was an older structure that pre-dated the roundhouse, and usually housed the smaller classes such as the 'Dollies' (F tanks) and Rx engines. Here Rx 222 awaits its next roster in August 1959.
Photo: M. Billett

new broad gauge class put into service on SAR. Were worked heavily during their lives (in some cases only 11 years) and fitted with Alco reversing gear were greatly valued for heavy shunting besides freight duties. This was the main reason for their gainful employment at Port Pirie on shunting duties in the 1960s. Though No.747 lingered around until 1966, no examples were saved for preservation.

750 class
Bought off the Victorian Railways (were originally their 'N' class Nos. 474, 471, 477, 465, 461, 485, 491, 494 and 495) from 1951 these North British 'light' Mikados were to fill a serious shortage of motive power together with the 740 class. The class was particularly useful in that they could work lines restricted to the larger Mikados, and at the same time had much more available tractive power than the other standard light lines alternative the Rx class. As a result a number of 750s were usually allocated to Tailem Bend for working the light Mallee lines, with Mile End locos working the Spalding and Truro branches. By the early 1960s, however, the class was all but stored though No. 752 (now preserved) was made useful on odd duties.

CLASS SPECIFICATIONS

Class	Builder	Number built	Years	Notation	Cylinders	Drive wheel	Boiler Pressure	Weight	Tractive Effort
P	Martin (14) Beyer-Peacock (6)	20	1884-1893	2-4-0T	16" x 20" (i)	5' 0"	145 lb	33.7 ton	10,520 lb
Rx	Dubs (6) Walkers (25) Martin (24) Islington (14) North British (15)	84	1899-1916	4-6-0	18" x 24"	4' 6"	175 lb	88.6 ton	21,420
2nd F	Islington (21) Martin (13) Perry (10)	44*	1902-1922	4-6-2T	17½" x 24"	5' 3"	185 lb	59 ton	18,340
S	Martin	18	1894-1904	4-4-0	18" x 24" (i)	6' 6"	150 lb	82.1 ton	12,710
500B	Armstrong-Whitworth	10	1926	4-8-4	26" x 28"	5' 3"	200 lb	222.3 ton	59,000
520	Islington	12	1943-1947	4-8-4	20½" x 28"	5' 6"	215 lb	200.65 ton	32,600
600C	Armstrong-Whitworth	10	1926	4-6-2	24" x 28"	6' 3"	215 lb†	196.95 ton	39,300
620	Islington	10	1936-1938	4-6-2	18½" x 28"	5' 6"	200 lb	140.75 ton	25,000
700	Armstrong-Whitworth	10	1926	2-8-2	22" x 28"	4' 9"	200 lb	171.15 ton	40,400
710	Islington	10	1932-1939	2-8-2	22" x 28"	4' 9"	200 lb	175.8 ton	40,400
720	Islington	17	1930-1943	2-8-4	22" x 28"	4' 9"	215 lb	227.4 ton	52,000
740	Clyde Engineering	10	1952-1953	2-8-2	22" x 28"	4' 9"	200 lb	165.05 ton	40,400
750	North British	10	1951	2-8-2	20" x 26"	4' 7¼"	175 lb	124.7 ton	28,650

NOTES: *This total includes the second No.244 which was rebuilt from the frame of No.239 (condemned in May 1956) and the boiler of the original No.244 (condemned in July 1956). This second No.244 entered traffic during May 1956.

†This class originally built with 200 lb sq. in. boilers, with the higher stress ones fitted from the late 1930s. Their original tractive effort was stated as 36,600 lb.

(i) indicates inside cylinders.

Rx197 drags a 'dead' 521 Thomas Playford through the loco yard at Mile End, February 17, 1966.   Photo: J. Wilson

Preserved '620' class pacific No. 621 with the post-steam name of Duke of Edinburgh returns to the roundhouse (by now empty) to use the turntable on May 6, 1972.   Photo: S. A. McNicol

Berkshire No. 729 was near the end of her useful life when this photo was taken about 1957 at Clapham, and the exceptionally short freight attached to her is testimony to oncoming obsolescence.   Photo: S.A. Archives

BIBLIOGRAPHY

In as many cases as possible official S.A.R. Mechanical Branch records have been used throughout this book. In addition the following have been used for reference and comparison.

Tuplin, W.A., *The Steam Locomotive,* Adams & Dart, Bath, 1974.
Nock, O.S., *The Railway Enthusiast's Encyclopaedia,* Hutchinson, London, 1968.
South Australian Railway's Institute Magazine, various issues 1957-68.
South Australian Government Railways (a public relations booklet), 1929.
A.R.H.S. South Australian Division, *The Recorder*, (various issues).
South Australian Railways, *General Appendix to the Rule Book*, 1948.
Marshall, B & Wilson, J, *Locomotives of the S.A.R.*, Mile End Railway Museum Publication, Adelaide, 1972.
South Australian Government, *Parliamentary Debates*, 1924-1931 inclusive.
Annual Report of the South Australian Commissioner, 1919-1931 inclusive.
Truck and Bus Transportation magazine, April/June/July-August/September and November 1940.
South Australian Railways, *Working Timetables*, June 1953 and September 1966.